Proportional Misr

For my parents, to whom I owe so much

Proportional Misrepresentation

The Case Against PR in Britain

Peter Hain

WILDWOOD HOUSE

Published by
Wildwood House Limited
Gower House, Croft Road
Hants GU11 3HR
England

ISBN 0 7045 3086 4 Case
ISBN 0 7045 0526 6 Limp

Printed and bound in Great Britain by
Biddles Ltd, Guildford and King's Lynn

Contents

PREFACE

Quite a few books and even more pamphlets on proportional representation and electoral reform have appeared in the 1970s and 1980s. All have been strongly pro-PR, and most have described the workings of alternative electoral systems in great, and at times excruciating, detail.

This book is different. It is not a pro-PR tract – indeed it challenges much of the case for proportional representation. It is also deliberately non-technical and many of the mysteries of different PR systems are not discussed. Instead it attempts to provide an accessible guide to the subject in the early chapters, a critical political discussion in the middle, and at the end a positive alternative programme of democratic reform. The notes are for reference purposes only and should not interrupt and flow of reading.

Much of the thinking in the book first surfaced in a pamphlet on the subject co-written with Geoff Hodgson in 1982, and I have drawn heavily on his insights then and his subsequent advice.

Additionally, I am grateful for their comments and advice to my father, Andy Batkin, Maggie Jones, Rab MacWilliam, Nigel Stanley and Jack Straw. Thanks also to Pat, Sam and Jake for their support and affection.

Peter Hain, Putney, April 1986.

1

A CASE TO ANSWER

Nobody can deny the validity of the cries 'unfair', 'foul' or 'antiquated' increasingly levelled at Britain's electoral system. It *is* unfair that smaller political parties are denied a share of parliamentary seats more equal to their share of the total vote. It *is* hard to defend a system which could produce a government with an overall majority on the basis of little more than a third of the popular vote.

First-past-the-post electoral systems can unquestionably result in all sorts of anomalies. Labour lost power in 1951 despite having nearly 1 per cent more of the popular vote than Churchill's Conservatives, and Labour won power in February 1974 despite having 1 per cent less votes than the Tories (though these two results were also affected by out-of-date boundaries). Mrs Thatcher gained a landslide majority in 1983 by winning 58 more seats than in the 1979 general election even though the Tory vote actually declined by 1.5 per cent.

In 1983 the Liberals and the Social Democrats together polled over 25 per cent of votes, but obtained under 4 per cent of MPs; it took:

32,777 votes to elect a Conservative MP
40,482 votes to elect a Labour MP
338,860 votes to elect an Alliance MP.

The winner-takes-all procedure also meant that over half of those who turned out to vote in 1983 may as well have stayed at home because their vote made no difference to the final result in their local constituency: across the whole country, 3 million Tory votes, 4 million Labour votes and 7 million Alliance votes were 'wasted' in this way.

These are just a few of the facts quoted by advocates of proportional representation (PR) to support their case for a fairer electoral system. On grounds of *fairness*, it is hard to deny their case: PR would produce a fairer distribution of seats. But to claim because of this that PR would be more *democratic* is altogether different, for most PR advocates fail to acknowledge the extent to which their alternatives would undermine important democratic principles.

Whilst this is not the place to attempt a full description of what is meant by 'democracy' (the term is deployed in a great variety of often contradictory ways), it should include several key principles. First, *accountability*: representatives must be made answerable to their electors in a more regular and direct way than can be achieved simply by periodic elections. Second, *participation*: each individual must be able to intervene directly in the political process and influence affairs, rather than leaving decision-making to representatives or political elites. Third, *decentralisation*: spreading power to local levels can diminish the tendency in almost any system towards bureaucratic and centralised control.

A fairer distribution of seats is desirable in a democratic system, but if it can only be achieved at the expense of those other ideals, then we are entitled to question the justification for pursuing it.

PR initiatives in Britain

Proportional representation has been pressed at various points in British history. As one political scientist has pointed out, PR 'has come to the fore as an issue in British politics only in periods when the party system itself is in flux'.[1] During this century there have been two main periods – 1906 to 1918 and since 1972 – when PR has been a major issue of public interest. The first period saw the rise of the Labour Party and the latter the re-emergence of the Liberals (subsequently buttressed by the Social Democratic Party or SDP. Both of these trends destabilised the previously entrenched two-party systems.

However, PR had surfaced before then. In 1857 the political thinker Thomas Hare first proposed the idea of transferable voting within a single constituency, either municipal or country-wide. But although he won the backing of John Stuart Mill, few others were interested. Mill's support was partly motivated by his fear of the 'tyranny of the majority', the fear 'that the coming of the wider franchise would usher in something like mob rule'.[2] By guaranteeing the election of at least a proportion of the 'civilised' and the educated, PR might act as a bulwark against the ignorant masses. However, Mill was also anxious to promote fairness, pointing out in a Commons debate in 1866 that: 'A class may have a great number of votes in every constituency in the Kingdom and not obtain a single representative in this House. Their right of voting may be only the right of being outvoted'.[3]

During the nineteenth century, the electoral system underwent a number of major changes, not least the widening of the franchise. Before the 1832 Reform Act there were 'double member' parliamentary seats, and afterwards many became three-membered seats. Then under the 1867 Reform Act a form of PR known as the 'limited vote' was introduced. In thirteen of the larger cities each elector was only able to cast two votes in the three-member constituencies, this device ensuring that parties in a minority in each city (e.g. the Tories in Manchester or the Liberals in Liverpool) retained some representation. The 1870 Education Act also included a limited form of PR in elections for school boards, in order to ensure representation on them of different religious interests.

But the 'limited vote' was abolished under the 1885 Reform Act, as were most multi-member seats; there was greater standardisation in the size of constituencies. By now the party system had asserted itself, with people voting mostly for national parties rather than individuals.

A Proportional Representation Society had been formed in 1884 (in 1959 it changed its name to the Electoral Reform Society, currently the most active PR group). But PR remained a minority concern for the next twenty years, until a combination of factors (including the introduction of PR elsewhere in Europe and the formation of the Labour Party) re-kindled interest in it.

The long dormant PR Society became active again in 1905. From then until 1918 there were a series of inquiries and parliamentary votes on the issue. Asquith set up a Royal Commission on Electoral Systems in 1908 and it reported in 1910. But it was unable to come to any clear verdict, favouring a 'Single Transferable' (STV) system of PR over a 'List' system, but narrowly rejecting it as a system suitable for the Commons. Somewhat equivocally, the Commission opted for a different method of electoral reform, the non-proportional Alternative Vote (AV) system.* Nothing came of this, partly because the Commission had been so cautious, and partly because the AV would have assisted a Labour Party which was by then beginning to challenge the Liberals.

Then a Speaker's Conference was established in 1916, reporting the following year. In 188 constituencies it favoured an STV system with three or more MPs in each 'multi-member' seat, and proposed that the Alternative Vote be deployed in the remaining 'single-member' seats. The recommendations were part of a package with many features (including the requirement for a parliamentary deposit and a residential basis of electoral registration) which have survived to this day. But during the subsequent parliamentary debate on what became the 1918 Representation of the People Act, neither PR nor the AV was accepted. The main Commons vote against PR was by 201 to 169, and the AV was also rejected after an impasse with the House of Lords.[4]

As a result, by 1920 Britain was the only democratic country in Western Europe not to have adopted some form of PR. A number of explanations have been advanced for this.[5] Britain was at the time less part of Europe than of the Anglo-Saxon world, where first-past-the-post voting dominated. The British Tory Party was stronger than its continental counterparts and had less to fear from the left, so it had no particular interest

* People vote 1, 2, 3 etc and winning candidates have to secure a majority of the vote after the second (and, if necessary, later) preferences of people who vote for the least popular candidates have been transferred: for a fuller description, see Chapter 7.

4

in electoral reform. There was also an accidental element in the many, and sometimes confusing, Commons votes on PR: majorities against PR were often small, falling to 8 on one occasion, and suggesting that if 'the proponents of both reforms [AV and STV] had been able to agree on one reform at a time, there would have been a majority'.[6]

After 1918, electoral reform became much more of a partisan matter. The Liberals formally adopted PR as a policy for the first time in their 1922 election manifesto, Labour moved away from its decision in 1918 to favour PR and the Tories had no reason to pursue it.

But in 1929 there was a further development. A Speaker's Conference was set up by the minority Labour government as part of a deal to secure parliamentary support from Lloyd George's Liberals. He had not insisted on the introduction of STV as the price for backing Labour, as he was more equivocal about PR than many others in his party. In the event, party interest again dictated the outcome of the Speaker's Conference. As has been explained:

> The Liberals wanted PR but would take the AV as second best; Labour wanted no change but was prepared to offer the AV; while the Conservatives rightly foresaw that the AV, which would mainly help second-place Liberals to win county seats from them, was their worst solution. So the conference made two majority recommendations: that the alternative vote should not be used (Conservative and Labour versus Liberal) and that any change in the electoral system should involve proportional representation (Conservative and Liberal versus Labour), which were duly ignored by the government since they reflected the wrong party combination.[7]

Labour introduced a Bill favouring the AV in 1931 and it was actually carried in the Commons by 295 votes (of whom 253 were Labour and 40 Liberals) to 230 (227 of whom were Tories). But it did not pass into law as it became snarled up in the Lords and then fell with the demise of Ramsay MacDonald's Labour administration in the crisis later that year. But this attempt to introduce the AV, though nearly successful, was to be the last major attempt to replace the first-past-the-post system until electoral reform appeared on the agenda again in the 1970s.

A democratic alternative

When it did so, however, the fact that there are many different systems of proportional representation was seldom spelt out to the public with the same force as the general case for PR.

The most widely canvassed for Britain is the Single Transferable Vote in multi-member constituencies. Another is the 'List' system used in some European countries. There is also the 'Additional Member' option proposed in 1976 by the Hansard Society.

As will be clear from subsequent chapters, each of these systems has advantages. But each has major disadvantages too: the key question, rarely addressed by PR supporters, is whether the disadvantages are so great as to undermine the very case for PR.

It is also important to note that those in favour of PR do not confine their arguments to electoral ones of natural justice. They make much bolder claims that PR would radically transform the whole economic and social system, unleashing new forces for prosperity and stability. To the more fervent campaigners, PR seems at times to be a cure-all for Britain's economic and social ills.

In fact, PR may well be a complete diversion: an alternative programme of radical political reform could extend and improve the quality of democracy far more effectively. Therefore, to question the case for PR is not to defend the *status quo*. It is common ground amongst those who hold progressive opinions – whether they are pro-PR, anti-PR or agnostic about it – that Britain's political system is antiquated, much too centralised, elitist and obsessively secretive. Far-reaching changes are necessary to make it genuinely democratic. Furthermore, if electoral reform is to be pursued as part of these changes, the 'Alternative Vote' system might satisfy the desire for fairness whilst protecting the other democratic principles which PR can be shown to undermine.

2

SINGLE TRANSFERABLE VOTING

The PR system commonly proposed for Britain is the Single Transferable Vote in multi-member constituencies (STV). Supported by the Liberals, the SDP and the Electoral Reform Society, the system has been used in the Republic of Ireland (since 1922), Malta (since 1921) and Tasmania (since 1907). It was also used for the short-lived Northern Ireland Assembly in 1973 and in the subsequent Assembly there from 1982.

It would replace our traditional single-member constituency averaging 65,000 electors with massive new constituencies averaging 315,000 electors. These would have four or five members: the greater the number of members, the greater the possibility of obtaining a closer proportionality between the representation of parties and their electoral support. In a seat with few members, there is obviously little scope for each party; with more members, the major parties have a good chance to win at least one seat.

Both the Alliance and the Electoral Reform Society have outlined how the new multi-member seats would be created by merging existing ones. For instance, a city like Edinburgh might have six members, a county like Cornwall five.

The major parties would probably run as many candidates as there were MPs for each of the new constituencies, and voters would mark their ballot papers in order of preference: 1, 2, 3 etc. They could confine their choice to the candidates from their preferred party; they could continue to express preferences right through the list for as many candidates of different parties as they wished; or they could vote for just one candidate.

Before the votes are counted, a 'quota' is calculated: the minimum number of votes a candidate needs to be elected. In a four-member seat, for example, the quota would be one-fifth of the votes cast plus one. If the total votes cast in a four-member constituency was 200,000, any candidate getting at least one more than one-fifth (i.e. 40,001) would be elected.*

Any candidate who got more than the quota in 'first preferences' would be elected right away. His or her votes in *excess* of the quota would then be transferred to other candidates in accordance with the second preferences marked on the ballot papers (see the Appendix for details). If no candidate reached the quota on the first count, then the candidate who got the lowest number of first preference votes would drop out, with *all* his or her second preferences transferring to others. This would continue with the next preferences of candidates at the top and the bottom being progressively redistributed until all the places were filled by candidates whose votes, totalled up by this process, passed the quota. The counting process is actually very complicated and the counts could take days rather than hours: a detailed discussion of the methods used can be found in the Appendix at the end of this book and in other studies of PR.[8]

The case for STV

The essential case for STV is that it ought to result in a fairer representation of parties in the House of Commons. In the 1983 election, for example, hundreds of thousands of votes cast for Labour in the South of England saw no Labour MP returned. A similar picture applied to Tory voters in inner-city areas: despite having significant electoral support there, the Conservatives failed to gain representation in Liverpool, Glasgow, the mining areas of South Wales and major areas of

* In this example the quota for victory is 40,000 plus one. The general mathematical formula for a quota is $\dfrac{n}{r+1} + 1$,

where n is the total votes cast and r the number of MPs in the multi-member constituency.

the industrial heartlands of Northern England. Alliance supporters saw their votes wasted across most of the country. Labour won nine times as many MPs despite having only 2 per cent more of the popular vote than the Alliance.

In recent elections in Britain about half the votes cast played no direct part in the election of an MP, whereas under STV this could be reduced to below a fifth. STV would end the practice whereby most MPs under the 'winner-takes-all' procedure are elected on a minority vote, with the majority of local electors voting for other parties. It would also mean less 'wasted' votes: in most five-member seats it is probable that each of the three major parties would get at least one seat.

Another argument advanced for STV is that it would allow electors to choose between different candidates *within* parties. Suppose that in a five-member seat where most voters were progressively inclined the Conservatives fielded two from the Party's extreme right, two from the centre and one outspoken person from its liberal wing. It is likely that if two of the elected members were Labour and two Alliance, then the fifth might be the 'liberal' Tory. Similarly, a candidate from any of the parties who was well-known for some reason – perhaps because of involvement in a popular local campaign – might do better.

The STV option is the most popular one amongst British PR supporters. However, they are by no means united on a common system of STV – there are almost endless variations. They have also been unable to overcome its main defect: the monster, multi-member constituencies it requires.

Monster constituencies

Five-member seats would have well over 300,000 electors. In London, for example, the average seat would be about one and a half times the size of an existing borough. But the average STV constituency would be even more unwieldy in rural areas, say Northern Scotland, where the seat would cover thousands of square miles of land and sea. Because of the problems associated with such large constituencies, a prestigious all-party and pro-PR commission set up by the Hansard Society recommended against the STV system in 1976. Its Report pointed out that in no case had STV been used in a country with a population anywhere near as great as Britain's.[9] In Ireland, for example, often cited favourably by STV supporters, the average five-member constituency has 70,000 electors, whereas in Britain it would be over four times that size.

One solution, retaining *existing* seats, but making them multi-member ones by multiplying (by, on average, four) the number of MPs in each, has also been dismissed by PR supporters: having a House of Commons with over 3,000 MPs is clearly impractical and democratically undesirable.

In an attempt to overcome some of these problems of STV, the Electoral Reform Society proposed a complex arrangement where seats would range from three members (in predominantly rural areas) to eight members (in the city of Leeds).[10] But while mitigating the problem, this did not overcome the central objection to large, amorphous constituencies in which it would be difficult for voters to identify with their MPs and even more difficult for MPs to reflect the views of distinct local communities.

Community PR

In July 1982 a joint Liberal/SDP Commission on Constitutional Reform launched proposals for a 'Community PR' system of STV consisting of 143 different sized constituencies formed by merging existing single-member seats.[11] Some would have as many as eight members, others as few as one, two or three. Most of the large ones would be in urban areas and the smaller ones in rural areas.

The objective of this option was to overcome the defects of a conventional STV system where each seat has a uniform number of members (usually 5), some are ridiculously large and geographically diverse and others bring together communities which have no natural identity of interest.

Community PR tries to create seats out of 'natural communities'. Single-member seats would be formed in scantily populated areas like Caithness and Sutherland in the Scottish Highlands, and on islands like the Isle of Wight and Orkney and Shetlands. Two-, three- or four-member seats would be formed in natural county or shire areas. Towns and cities would become single seats with the number of members being determined by their population: Hull and Plymouth would be three-member, Coventry four-member, Bristol five-member, Sheffield six-member, Liverpool seven-member and Leeds eight-member.

However, community PR would simply substitute one set of idiosyncracies for another. Conveniently, three of the four proposed single-member seats were held at the time by Alliance MPs. Amongst the multi-member seats suggested were a number where an extra MP was added in a way which seemed designed to ensure that the Alliance benefited.

'Community PR' would treat the major parties unevenly in another respect. Most rural seats would have four or less MPs and on recent performances it would be difficult for the Labour Party to gain representation there, even if it polled over 20 per cent. By contrast, if the Alliance and Tories polled under 20 per cent in the urban seats with more members, they would be certain to secure at least one MP. Thus Community PR would be politically discriminatory.

Anomalies under STV

Although it would introduce a much fairer distribution of MPs, it would not introduce full proportionality, which can only be obtained with a system of large and uniform multi-member seats. The optimal number of members for an STV system is generally considered to be five: a smaller number allows the strongest local party to gain disproportionately, while a larger number increases the degree of proportionality by only a small degree. Thus the *member size* of individual constituencies can have a crucial effect on the national outcome of a general election.

In a five-member constituency the quota needed to get elected is one-sixth of the vote. In a three-member constituency the quota is higher: a quarter of the vote. A party which is weak in a three-member seat will therefore be under-represented compared with one which is weak in a five-member seat. Since the evidence suggests that three-member seats benefit the local majority party disproportionately, and since they are proposed mainly in rural areas, the Conservatives would be favoured.

Furthermore, where a party (such as has been the case with the Alliance) has support which tends to be evenly spread rather than concentrated in particular areas (as, for instance, with Labour in urban areas), it could find itself under-represented.

For example, across the whole of the 25 three-member constituencies proposed under Community PR, a party could win just under 25 per cent of the vote and yet receive no representation at all. In the 29 four-member seats parties averaging just under 20 per cent would similarly be without representation. In the 1983 election this would certainly have penalised both the Alliance and Labour, albeit in different areas.

The departure from strict proportionality required by the practical implementation of an STV system can produce some odd results. In Malta in 1981 the Nationalists won 50.9 per cent of first-preference votes, yet gained only 31 seats (compared with Labour's 34 seats on 49.1 per cent of first-preference votes). However, this had not occurred before in 60 years and would seem to be a problem peculiar to a country with two closely competing parties and a relatively small number of constituencies, which is not the case in Britain.[12]

Ireland's STV system, with its mix of three-member, four-member and five-member constituencies, has also produced some odd results. In 1965 and 1969 Fianna Fail gained an overall parliamentary majority with under half the votes – less than the combined opposition coalition of Fine Gael/Labour. Yet in 1973, despite getting a higher vote than in 1969, Fianna Fail was swept out of office by Fine Gael/Labour, who actually polled a lower share of the vote than they had in 1965 or 1969. Additionally, the Labour Party has had the galling experience of increasing its share of the vote, yet losing seats (as happened between 1965 and 1969, for instance). There are various complicated reasons for these distortions.[13]

One factor was that Ireland was notorious for the boundaries of three-member seats being 'gerrymandered'. Until 1980 the government of the day had responsibility for redrawing boundaries to fit shifting population trends. Fianna Fail were responsible for revisions in 1935, 1947, 1961 and 1969, which tried to establish three-member seats where it was strong, four-member seats where it was weak, and tried to reduce the number of five-member seats to a minimum. However, when it came to the turn of the Fine Gael/Labour coalition to revise boundaries in 1974, the minister responsible, James Tully, implemented changes which backfired in favour of Fianna Fail at the subsequent election of 1977 (hence the birth of the term 'Tullymander', i.e. a failed gerrymander).

The 1984 European elections showed how far short of proportionality Ireland's STV system could fall. The Labour Party polled 8 per cent yet did not get a seat, although in strict proportional terms it would have been entitled to one on only 6.6 per cent. Fianna Fail with 39 per cent of the vote got 53 per cent of seats, while Fine Gael with 32 per cent of votes got 40 per cent of seats.

The Irish experience also underlines another problem of STV: that of by-elections. They are held using the Alternative Vote and, with only one member to be elected, it is impossible to achieve true proportionality. Because of this, if the MP retiring or deceased is from a minority party, it is likely to lose its representation.

Far from STV boosting the prospects of minority parties, as is often claimed, they would have to overcome fairly high hurdles to secure an MP: even in five-member seats (of which there would be 48 under community PR), the minimum vote necessary would be 17 per cent. In Ireland three parties – Fianna Fail, Fine Gael and Labour – have dominated representation in the Dail despite STV. In Malta only the two major parties are represented in parliament.

The conflict between the desire to have small constituencies and the desire to achieve greater proportionality is inherent in the multi-member STV system. This is evident in the way the Community PR option would work. Its attempt to overcome

13

the problems of the larger STV constituencies by reducing member sizes in many areas produces other distortions and reduces the scope for securing full proportionality.

It is therefore important to bear in mind that although the first-past-the-post system has plenty of anomalies, STV has its own share too, which could produce eccentric general election results. It is fairer in some ways but unfair in others, raising the question of democratic *priorities* which will be addressed in Chapter four.

3

'LIST' OR 'MIXED' SYSTEMS OF PR

Concerned at the complexities and anomalies of STV, some PR supporters are in favour of what are called 'List' systems. Basically, voters vote for a party rather than an individual, and MPs are then selected from central or regional party lists of candidates in numbers proportional to their party's total vote.

National List systems operate in Israel, Guyana and Turkey. Since the founding of the State of Israel in 1948, the country has effectively voted as a single constituency, albeit with electoral areas for purposes of registration and voting. It returns 120 MPs chosen from national lists of candidates drawn up by each party and ranked in order of preference.

The main advantage of the Israeli system is that it achieves both a high degree of proportionality and a higher ratio of 'effective' votes than even STV: in the 1974 Israeli elections, for example, 96 per cent of the votes cast were effective in securing a winning candidate (compared with around 50 per cent in Britain's elections the same year).

The Belgians were the first to adopt a List system in 1899, partly to overcome friction between their Flemish and Walloon peoples: the system ensured both would be fairly represented and this eased tension. It was later introduced elsewhere in Europe.

Regional list systems

But in Western Europe the List systems adopted have not

been national ones, since these concentrate power in the national party organisations which govern the selection and order of preference of candidates on the lists. Regionally-based systems operate in Austria, Belgium, Iceland, Italy, the Netherlands, Luxembourg, Norway, Sweden, Denmark, Finland and Switzerland. These allow for greater local accountability because the party lists are chosen on a regional basis.

Although the List system sounds simple in theory, this is not usually the case in practice. Most of the regional systems are divided into multi-member constituencies, and the votes cast rarely divide neatly into the seats available. As a result, different formulae have been introduced to calculate the allocation of seats – some help larger parties, some smaller ones, and others try to find a middle way; ballot forms and counting procedures can also be extremely complicated.[14]

Other anomalies abound. For instance, urban voters in Norway are under-represented (compared with rural voters) because of the size of the constituencies and the way they are arranged. To overcome this, several countries (Sweden and Denmark, for instance) have created a 'pool' of seats which are allocated when the counting has been completed, to even up the result and ensure that as close as possible a proximity of seats to votes is achieved. There is also less opportunity for public opinion to make itself felt between general elections because there are no by-elections under List systems: the vacancy is simply filled by the next candidate on the list.

Obviously, the fact that a different system is complex does not invalidate it as an alternative to Britain's one: if other people have managed, there is no reason why the British couldn't too.

The real objections to List systems are ones which have led most British supporters of PR to reject them. First, the link between the MP and the local constituents is completely broken. Second, power is further centralised by concentrating decision-making over the selection of candidates, and thereby the allocation of seats, into national (or, at best, regional) party organisations. Local community and even local party opinion can be virtually shut out under this arrangement.

The German system

An attempt to strike a compromise is found in Germany. Here, proportionality is achieved by 'topping up' a single-member constituency system with a list system. Each elector has two votes. The first is for the 'constituency candidate', chosen on the same basis as in Britain. The second is for the party. Usually voters choose the party to which the candidate they have supported belongs, but they need not do so.

Half the seats are filled by 'constituency MPs' elected on the first-past-the-post basis. The other half are allocated by a computer to candidates on regional party lists to top up their total number of MPs to an amount that is directly proportional to their overall standing in the second or 'party' vote aggregated across each region. There is a 'threshold' vote of 5 per cent which parties have to pass before they are entitled to representation.

In some respects preferable to other List systems, the German one nevertheless suffers from a number of disadvantages. The first-past-the-post constituency element still returns MPs who do not have to win a majority of the local electorate, offending one of the principles most keenly adhered to by PR supporters. The list element of the system is controlled by party bureaucracies and is vulnerable to patronage: the great virtue of local party control is that the scope for patronage and central manipulation is limited. As one of Britain's leading PR advocates, Enid Lakeman, concedes: 'It is nearly impossible for the German voters to elect a person whom the Party organisation does not want, and quite impossible to reject one whom the party does want.'[15]

When it considered the implications of introducing a German-type system in Britain, the 1976 (pro-PR) report of the Hansard Society was especially concerned about the implications of having two types of MPs: those elected as now and those who need not have the substantial support of electors in any area but are appointed by the party machine. Directly elected MPs could claim to be more legitimate than those appointed, and the system means a substantial body in Parliament would not be democratically accountable to the electorate.

17

It is sometimes claimed that the German system has the advantage over Britain's of a more personal element to voting. The two-vote procedure does give electors the opportunity both to vote for their party and thereby contribute to its total regional support, whilst also plumping for a particular candidate they might favour even if he or she is not the nominee of the party supported by that voter. In practice, however, 'its personal element is illusory . . . successful candidates are those whom their parties nominate for the safest seats or as heads of lists. The German voter . . . if he wishes to support a party but considers some other candidate personally superior to his party's nominee in his constituency . . . can use his first vote for that other candidate without affecting the total party representation. However, very little use is made of this and there is reason to think that many voters do not understand the functions of their two votes. In most constituencies the candidates' first votes are nearly the same as the second votes cast for their parties.'[16]

Implemented in Britain, the German system would mean either doubling the size of the present parliamentary constituencies or doubling the number of MPs to 1,300. There are serious democratic objections to doubling constituency sizes: the remoteness of MPs from their constituents and their parties would be increased. There are major practical objections to doubling the number of MPs: the House of Commons would have to be rebuilt (with a new chamber twice the size and vast new back-up facilities) and the boundary commissioners would have to embark on another review lasting several years at least. Doubtless such practical objections could be ignored if a qualitative improvement in democracy was secured, but there is no reason for supposing that this would be the case.

Additional member system

The Hansard report opted instead for a further compromise option which it termed the 'Additional Member' system. The Hansard Society had convened a commission of eminent people from public life, chaired by the Oxford historian, Lord Blake. On it were leading academics, MPs from each party, peers, and top businesspeople. Although its ethos was pro-PR, it was not constrained by partisan interests and its analysis was dispassionate – a feature noticeably absent from most other literature on the subject. The resulting report is therefore of special interest.

As has been pointed out, the report rejected both the STV and List systems. Its proposal for an Additional Member option was quite new. Under this, electors would vote exactly as they do now, filling three-quarters of the seats (480), except that they would be increased in size by about a third. The remaining quarter (160) would be used to 'top up' these seats, as in the German system, to achieve greater proportionality within each region of the country. In other words, the directly elected MPs would be supplemented by others in order to ensure that the number of seats in the regions corresponded as closely as possible to the proportion of votes cast for each party.

The main difference from the German system is that the additional seats would not go to party appointees, but to the most successful of the losing candidates in the constituency elections: thus each MP would have had to gain some significant electoral support, which is not necessarily the case in Germany. There would be a similar threshold vote of 5 per cent. Using this system, the commission projected an October 1974 election result as follows:

	Additional Member System	Actual Result	'True' Proportionality
Labour	255	319	249
Tory	245	277	227
Liberal	105	13	116

But it is significant that, despite its prestige and its dispassionate approach, the Hansard Report came up with an option suffering from major shortcomings. It still recommended two classes of MPs, those directly elected and those 'additional' members. Some constituencies would have two or maybe even three MPs; other constituencies would have just one MP. The 'additional' MPs need have no connection with the area to which they are allocated. On the basis of doing relatively well in another area, a candidate would be allocated as an additional member to a seat where he or she might actually be unpopular. To claim, therefore, that there is a compensating factor in that, unlike in Germany, the additional members need at least to have won some electoral support is rather misleading, for the particular electors they find themselves representing need not have had a say in who they are.

There is also an element of pure chance affecting the choice of the additional member. Losing candidates in seats where their party came a good second or third would find themselves 'representing' other seats as additional members, not on the basis of their own particular merits, but on the basis of the electoral support their party enjoyed in the seat in which they stood, and this could in turn depend on how many other parties were standing there and competing for a share of the vote.

The system is not fully proportional and, by increasing the size of constituencies, would both increase the remoteness of MPs and require a complex boundary revision (the Community PR system of STV proposed aggregating existing seats, thereby avoiding the time-consuming process of drawing up fresh boundaries).

In its conclusions the Hansard commission was caught between a 'fundamental and unanimous' *desire* for electoral reform, and an honest acknowledgment that when it came to their actual *implementation* in Britain, all the PR options proposed had major, and in some cases fatal, defects. In that sense it expressed rather neatly the dominant dilemma of those who readily concede that the present system has shortcomings but who remain sceptical that democracy will be enhanced by adopting any of the alternatives so far proposed.

4

DEMOCRATIC PRIORITIES

Would any of the main PR systems actually improve the quality of British democracy? As was readily conceded in earlier chapters, they would each produce a fairer representation of parties and eliminate many of the anomalies of first-past-the-post. But this could only be achieved by introducing other anomalies. Additionally, it is by no means obvious that PR would be more democratic; a key issue in assessing this is the effect of PR on local accountability, an important yardstick for judging a modern democracy.

Up until the late eighteenth century political theory treated democracy as being equivalent to 'direct' democracy in the tradition of the *polis* in ancient Greece and later of Rousseau, where each citizen was supposed to participate and where there were no representatives in the modern sense. However, by the mid-nineteenth century elected legislatures emerged: these amounted to systems of 'indirect' or 'representative' democracy and provided an attractive alternative, especially in an age where the small city-state had been replaced by the large nation-state.

It is generally assumed that, in the words of one political scientist, 'the difference between direct and indirect democracy is radical . . . In direct democracy there is continuous participation of the people in the direct exercise of power, whereas indirect democracy amounts to a system of *limitation* and *control* of power.'[17] And the fact that electing representatives necessarily limits the extent to which popular participation is feasible is often used to argue that a system based upon decision-making by *elected* political elites is democratic – indeed that it is a central feature of the modern concept of democracy.

But if the objective is to create a society in which each citizen has the maximum feasible opportunity to have a real say in the decision-making process – an objective which ought to distinguish the genuine from the phoney democrat – then the question becomes how to reconcile more participatory or 'direct' democratic procedures with a representative system. This question will be discussed more fully in the last chapter.

For the moment, however, the focus is upon the *electoral* arrangements. One method of opening up more avenues for popular participation within the representative system is to make those elected more accountable to their electors, not simply at periodic elections but between them as well. If citizens cannot *themselves* participate directly in the decision-making process, then a minimum requirement for a democracy is surely that they should have as direct as possible an influence on *their MPs or councillors*.

Several criteria are relevant in assessing accountability. Local people must have good *information*, both about the activities and the policies of their representatives. They should have opportunities to be *consulted* wherever possible. For people to be able to make their views felt and monitor the performance of their representatives, electors and elected must also be in reasonably *close physical proximity*.

Additionally, through the party system at the very least, there should be mechanisms by which citizens can make their MPs answerable in a more realistic and effective way than merely at an election every few years. This means being able to *re*-select or *de*-select MPs before they have to face the electorate. On polling day the pressures to vote against political opponents and for the party one supports tend to predominate over the quality of the particular party candidate. If there is no effective means of re-selection, then accountability is undermined and the representative system can be democratic only to a limited degree.

Britain's constituency system

One of the main features of Britain's electoral system is that each Member of Parliament represents a geographical constituency with about 65,000 electors. Some are formed out of distinct communities, others are sections of cities or rural areas. However, they share the advantage of having an MP who has the opportunity to establish a clearly identifiable link with the local electorate; the latter can thus keep itself informed about the MP's activities.

This is obviously an important element in a responsive system of democracy and the very name given to Britain's democratic parliamentary chamber underlines it. 'Commons' derives not from 'common', but from *commune*; in other words, it was meant to signify the national chamber where all the local communities are represented.

Admittedly the average size of British parliamentary constituencies is somewhat arbitrary and no case has been presented to suggest otherwise. Nor is it being suggested that they are of an optimal size for effective representation. The evidence shows that British MPs are still remote from their constituents and, as a vehicle for democratic participation and accountability, the system fails in important respects. But it is not being argued that the British system is perfect: far from it. The issue is whether PR would diminish even the limited opportunities currently given for local people to have real influence both over their local MP and the national government, and whether it would thwart attempts to extend those opportunities.

Party organisation

In Britain, constituency parties are important bodies. They are formed within the boundaries of parliamentary seats and contain local branches based upon local council wards. In the case of Labour, the Tories and the Liberals (though not the SDP, which has an area-based structure), the constituency party has the function of selecting the parliamentary candidate.

23

The person chosen is usually ratified by the national party as a matter of course.

In the Labour Party, recent reforms have boosted local influence. By ensuring that MPs have to undergo a mandatory process of re-selection by their local parties during each parliamentary session, and by establishing an electoral college which gives each constituency party a vote in the election of the national leader and deputy, party representatives are made more accountable to those who work to elect them.

As the recent history of the Labour Party shows, this has encouraged the more active involvement of ordinary members in their parties, thereby strengthening the democratic process. And partly because party members usually place a high premium upon performing casework effectively, being involved locally and reflecting local interests, MPs have been encouraged to be more sensitive to local community opinion and not simply to the local party as such.

Although Labour has gone furthest in this regard, there has been a more widespread assertion of the rights of local parties across the political spectrum. The very role of the constituency party has been enhanced over the past decade. The candidate or MP selected is encouraged to be in touch with not only the views of local party activists, but grass-roots opinion in general and the problems of the local area.

In that way constituency parties can act as counterweights to national or regional party bureaucracies. Although it would be misleading to overstate the impact of this, they can be one of the few forces pulling against the strong centralising tendencies within the party system, where an enormous amount of power and patronage is vested in the parliamentary leadership.[18]

Local accountability under PR

The major defect of PR is that, whatever system is adopted, the scope for local accountability is undermined, and more power is sucked upwards to regional or national levels of the party structure.

Under STV the influence of the ordinary party member –

small enough as it is – would be still further reduced. In multi-member seats, the selection of candidates would be done on an area rather than a constituency basis and power would shift away from the constituency level to area-based caucuses and party factions. The MP would have no clear line of accountability to the membership – unless local parties were merged to coincide with the areas covered by multi-member constituencies (which would itself be a centralising move). With fewer direct lines to individual local activists and members, MPs would find it more difficult to keep in touch. With the scope reduced for individual participation, MPs would also be more vulnerable under re-selection to being jettisoned through precisely the kind of factional manoeuvres most PR advocates so loudly denounce.

Under List systems candidates will have to be known outside their local areas to be voted onto the party list, and those supported by party officials and organisers would have a head start. And although under the Additional Member system the 'topping up' procedure may preserve many single-member constituencies, these will still be a third larger in order to make room for the additional members in the Commons. The MPs elected through any sort of list (with or without a topping-up element) will be chosen on a national, or at best, a regional basis. Their natural attachment will be to the party machine or the parliamentary leadership, rather than to local opinion.

This was evident in France when a new List system was introduced for the general election of March 1986. It gave party hierarchies a dominant role in choosing candidates and as a result weakened local interests. Party headquarters were able to draw up lists to ensure that leading figures were at the top and were thus certain to be elected. This produced battles between national, regional and local parties. Many local candidates had to give up their places to what were called 'parachutes' from Paris. Many national figures stood in areas where they had no local roots. In one case, the Socialist Culture Minister, a Parisian, found himself heading a list in one of the deepest rural areas of the country, and had to admit he knew nothing about agriculture. In many areas local parties drew up rival lists, and confusion was widespread: more than 7,000 candidates stood in 1986 compared with 2,700 in the previous election in May 1981. Another effect of this List system was to deprive not just local party members but local voters of any real choice. Taking account of opinion polls, one magazine published a month in advance the names of 448 candidates who were certain to be elected: only 129 out of 577 seats were seriously in doubt. This prediction proved extremely accurate.

Under the STV system with its massive constituencies (roughly five times larger than the present ones), it would be almost impossible for the MP to develop a close or informed relationship with his or her constituents. Close contact with constituency issues, individual electors and members of the local party would be difficult if not impossible – as British Euro-MPs have found in the similar sized single constituencies they represent.

Admittedly, such contact leaves a lot to be desired at present. A survey sponsored by Granada TV in 1972 found that four out of five electors were unable to mention anything their MP had done for their constituency, and half were unaware of their MP's name; the evidence also suggests that MPs make significant contact with only 10 to 15 per cent of their constituents.[19] But under STV this is bound to get much worse, as impediments of time, distance and organisation grow up between MPs and localities.

Surveys have shown a consistent desire by people to have an MP who plays an active role in looking after constituency matters, represents local issues and gives advice and support over individual problems. While people recognise that MPs have an important function in determining national policies, the evidence is that they want their MPs to be more locally involved than is usually the case.[20]

There is an argument against the notion of the MP as a 'local ombudsman'. One PR advocate suggests that too much emphasis on local involvement diverts MPs from their national role in controlling and influencing governments, and that many of the problems dealt with by MPs ought properly to be handled by local councillors.[21] But close local links and daily contact with individual problems encourage MPs to keep in touch with their constituents' lives and discourage them from being sucked into the remote atmosphere of Westminster. Any conflict of priorities between local and national functions should be resolved by improving back-up resources and facilities for MPs, not by downgrading their local links. And the proposition that MPs' caseloads can be pushed onto councillors ignores the fact that the latter are even more hard-pressed and under-resourced; it also ignores the fact that people are more likely to know how to contact their MP than their local councillor.

Although it is argued by its supporters that STV would at least allow residents to approach the MP representing the party they support, in practice they may be so physically distant from the MP that this alleged advantage would count for little. It is important to remember that STV has not operated anywhere else with a population as large as Britain's. The MP may not be able to keep his or her eye on the range of local issues concerned, and the electors may find it difficult to track down the MP of their choice. (Those who find this latter argument hard to accept reveal a marked ignorance about political realities, especially for the poorest members of the community who find even the present system consists of a series of obstacles needing to be overcome before they reach their MP, let alone obtain the service they require.)

There is also likely to be some conflict between MPs in the same multi-member seats in deciding how their roles will differ. Will they seek to represent their own party supporters only? Or will they divide up the whole constituency, and take a section each? This will probably vary according to local circumstances and the attitudes of the local parties and individuals concerned. But however demarcation lines are drawn, there are bound to be difficulties. On their own these would be relatively insignificant if the argument for STV was overwhelming, but that is not the case.

Another pro-STV argument suggests that because almost all of the multi-member constituencies would be 'marginal' in the sense that at least the fifth seat would be closely contested, MPs would have to be more responsive to local views.[22] But this is an assertion for which there is no supporting evidence and, even if true, it is hard to see how this would overcome the other substantial barriers producing greater remoteness.

The argument that STV promotes a fair spread of MPs in each seat has to be balanced against the fact that a candidate whom the most people showed they *positively wanted* need not top the poll. A candidate who achieved more first preferences than anyone else could be overtaken by candidates who were the first choice of less people but who were the second or third choice of more people. It is even conceivable for a candidate who got most first preferences to fail to get elected.

Coalition government

Another consequence of PR would be a greater likelihood of coalition governments. These, it is argued, would be beneficial because they would be more likely to reflect majority opinion. But this is by no means as clear-cut an issue as PR advocates often suggest.

There have been 23 general elections this century and in 17 of these the outcome has been an overall majority of MPs for a single party. But in only three of the 23 elections has one party obtained an overall majority of the total vote. And, on the assumption that the chosen PR system would have awarded seats in direct proportion to votes cast, there would have been minority or coalition governments on 20 out of 23 occasions.

Yet there is no guarantee that PR would have produced governments which reflected movements in opinion or class changes over this time. The two most outstanding shifts in party performance during the first half of the century were the rise in the Labour vote and the fall in the Liberal vote, shown by examining the key election results:

	Labour vote	*Liberal vote*
1900	1.8%	44.6%
1906	5.9%	49.0%
1910	7.6%	43.2%
1923	30.5%	29.6%
1929	37.1%	23.4%
1945	47.8%	9.0%
1951	48.8%	2.5%

The 'first-past-the post' system ensured that the major shifts in party allegiance were roughly reflected in the type of government that came to power. Labour did not hold office until the inter-war period, and then only with two minority governments. The Liberals achieved an overall majority in 1906 and participated in government, on a minority or coalition basis, continuously until 1922. They were also part of national or coalition governments from 1931 to 1945.

Since the Second World War, there have been five Labour governments, though as Labour's support started to tail off in the 1970s it formed one minority government (February to October 1974), followed by one (1974 to 1979) which survived its last two years only with Liberal support. Similarly, as the Liberal vote started to rise again from the early 1960s, the prospect of their participation in government rose, as shown in the 1977-8 pact with Labour. The emergence of a three-party system in the 1980s is likely to produce more minority governments, or pacts and coalitions involving the Alliance.

On the whole, therefore, movements in opinion since 1900 have been reflected, albeit crudely and with shortcomings, in the pattern of government. Although it is difficult to say what might have happened under PR, parallel shifts in the composition of governments to reflect ebbs and flows in public opinion would not necessarily have occurred.

To illustrate this, let us assume the same voting figures but with some form of *directly* proportional system. The Tories get more than half the vote in 1900 and therefore govern alone. In 1906 the Liberals and Labour together get more than half the vote and form a coalition government. They stay in power by means of a series of coalitions, after several elections with substantially the same total of Liberal-Labour votes (albeit with the balance between them altering) until 1931. Then there is a period of one-party Tory rule until 1945. After 1945 the Tories form a coalition government with the Liberals and others, excluding Labour entirely despite its massive 47.8 per cent vote. The Tories and Liberals then rule together without additional support from 1950 until at least the mid-1980s.

The purpose of this illustration is not to argue that this precise series of outcomes would actually have occurred, nor is it to deny that voting patterns would probably change under a different voting system. It is to underline the important point that PR does not necessarily permit changes in the distribution of the popular vote to be reflected in the composition of a government. In fact, it is generally *less* sensitive to *changes* in public opinion than the first-past-the-post system. Given that in Britain the 'core' votes of the major parties do not alter in the medium term, switches in governments are produced by switches in the allegiance of those who do change their minds.

However, as has been acknowledged already, there is an element of a gamble in Britain's winner-takes-all procedure. For instance, Labour's victory in 1964 with an overall majority of just 4 seats depended upon a 7-vote lead in Brighton Kemptown and a 27-vote lead in Ealing North. The four-seat majority could have disappeared if 4 and 14 (respectively) Labour voters in the two constituencies had voted Tory instead.[23] But a PR-elected government could equally have depended upon such small margins and vagaries of the electoral system. At least the British system is sensitive to changes in public opinion to an extent that a PR alternative might well not be.

The crucial point is that under PR one votes primarily for a *party* rather than for a *government*. Because coalitions are less likely under the existing system there is a much larger chance that party-directed votes will determine the complexion of the government. Once coalitions become the norm rather than the exception, the ordinary voter will have less opportunity to determine the composition of the government.

Centralised party deals

In general, the voter does not vote for a particular *combination* of parties to form a coalition. The voter does not express a preference indicating with which, if any, party his or her favoured party should coalesce. The coalition may in some general way reflect the balance of votes, but it is determined by a political deal done at the centre, not by the people voting in their local polling booths.

30

The only exception would be circumstances where two parties agreed in advance of an election to form a coalition afterwards, as has happened in West Germany for instance. Even then, the German experience illustrates the shortcomings of such pre-election agreements. In 1980 the German equivalent of Britain's Labour Party, the Social Democrats, formed a majority government with the German Liberals, the Free Democrats (FDP), who had told the electorate they would support the Social Democrats. Two years later, however, the FDP changed its mind. Without consulting the electorate, they simply switched sides, voted out the Social Democrats and formed a coalition with the Christian Democrats to put in a new right-wing government. The FDP has been described as 'the universal harlot of the German system; always in the governmental bed with the highest bidder'.[24] It has failed to win a single constituency by a simple majority since 1957 yet has been in government for all but three years during this period.

Nor is there any guarantee that inter-party deals will move in the direction of changes in popular opinion. It is even conceivable that a radical party could be pushed out of power as its vote *increased*. This has actually happened under PR systems elsewhere in Europe. It would be difficult in such circumstances to claim that PR was more democratic.

Suppose, for example, that at a future general election the following result occurred:

Labour	190 seats
Conservative	240 seats
Alliance	170 seats

Obviously this is a hypothetical, though not unrealistic, outcome. Perhaps less realistic but still possible, a coalition is formed between Labour and the Alliance. Then at the next election the result is:

Labour	250 seats
Conservative	190 seats
Alliance	160 seats

Labour has increased its share of the vote and its MPs, but there is no guarantee that it will remain in power. Perhaps because of a leftward shift within the party, the Alliance and

31

the Tories form a coalition this time, despite having both lost ground. Such 'contra-electoral' shifts in government would be quite possible under PR, the major beneficiaries being the centre parties rather than the people.

Centre parties benefit

Indeed centre parties usually hold the balance of power under PR. Unless one party can secure an overall majority, coalitions become the norm. Since it is unlikely that major parties from the left and right would agree to form a coalition (an exception being Germany's 'Grand Coalition' between the Christian Democrats and Social Democrats from 1966 to 1969), both would be inclined to seek common ground with forces in the centre. In this way centre parties can find themselves in government almost permanently, as in West Germany where the Free Democrats have been in government more than either of the major parties since the War despite having under 10 per cent of the vote.

This process has also tended to work against the left. In Italy, for instance, the main opposition party, the Communists, have won 30 to 32 per cent of votes consistently since 1948. Yet they have been excluded from government mainly because a variety of small centre parties (with a total of around 20 per cent) have coalesced with the Christian Democrats, who have remained in power, although only once winning an overall majority, since the War. In a similar way the centre-right has also benefited in Holland.

Those from the centre who are such avid supporters of PR claim that, by being in 'the middle', they are somehow more representative of the popular consensus and that it would therefore be more democratic if they were almost permanently in power within a shifting series of coalition administrations. But there is no evidence that their 'middle way' is especially popular. Simply because centrism might claim to offend less people does not mean it actually attracts support. It is likely to produce a 'lowest common denominator' type of government – one with a minimalist programme around which there is the least disagreement – rather than one which is positively supported by a significant section of the people. Perhaps for this reason, a National Opinion Poll in October 1985 found the public distinctly cool about a coalition. In answer to the question 'Do you think a coalition government would be good or bad for the country?', 37 per cent said 'Good', 46 per cent 'Bad' and 16 per cent 'Don't know'.

Because PR is likely to produce inconclusive results, with no party gaining an outright majority, the experience of other countries should be noted. It shows that the 'wheeler-dealing' which goes on behind the scenes can be far from satisfactory.

Take recent elections in Israel. After an inconclusive result in 1981, for example, there were protracted negotiations by both main parties with various minority groups to cobble together a parliamentary majority. Apart from creating a period of uncertainty in the country, the result was to give disproportionate power to tiny parties. As it happens, most of them have been on the right. But this is beside the point. How can it be claimed that PR improves the quality of democracy when minority parties can obtain such a potentially decisive influence?

In Europe, many countries regularly find themselves in the hands of 'caretaker' governments when it proves difficult to surmount the obstacles to forming a majority government. The Netherlands, Belgium and Italy have all been without effective governments for periods of weeks or months – for as long as seven months in the Netherlands in 1977. After the Dutch election in May 1981, it took nearly four months to form a coalition government which lasted just eight months; then followed three weeks of negotiations before another coalition was formed, which itself lasted only four months before facing a general election in September 1982. Ireland, often cited favourably by PR enthusiasts, has also experienced such periods of uncertainty. In one case the short-lived Fianna Fail government of 1982 survived only with the support of several independent MPs, one of whom managed to extract a promise of major public expenditure in his constituency as the price of his support. Around this time the country had three general elections in 18 months before a relatively stable government was formed.

Abandoning the manifesto

The PR lobby often stresses the opportunity under STV to vote for *individuals*, and that this produces a more 'personal' electoral procedure which is 'the essence of democracy'.[25] The claim is that electors would be able to vote for candidates they wished positively to support, rather than being lumbered with someone from their preferred party holding views they opposed. It is also suggested that 'independently minded' candidates might succeed. In fact the evidence shows that party discipline remains the overwhelming factor in transferring the second or later preferences of voters: there is little scope for independently-based candidates or strong personalities to break through the habit of voting according to party discipline.[26]

Notwithstanding these claims, however, PR advocates frequently ignore the democratic right of electors to vote for a set of *policies*. Under the present electoral system, the party manifesto at least symbolises the intentions of the party seeking to form a government. These intentions may not be implemented, and very few electors actually read the manifesto itself. But its general contents are widely publicised and, if people wish to, they are able to determine what they are voting for – and able to measure subsequent performance against manifesto promises.

Under PR – with its built-in tendency towards coalitionism – the manifesto is very unlikely to express the programme of the subsequent government. Parties will have to abandon or alter large sections of their manifestos as part of the compromise needed to form a coalition. The manifesto would become less a series of promises to be enacted, and more a set of trading tokens to be 'cashed' in exchange for political office. There will also be a temptation to add certain policies to the manifesto in the knowledge that, although other parties will find them unacceptable, they will make useful tokens with which to bargain for power after the election. Manifestos would become almost pointless, certainly as documents against which governments could later be assessed.

This will increase what is already a deep cynicism about

politicians' promises and party pre-election commitments. Whilst under the present system governments often abandon their promises, such behaviour would become the norm under PR. Under the present system, when manifesto commitments are abandoned, the governing party pays a price, usually in terms of lost support. With PR, no such price would be payable, because voters would rarely be given a *clear choice* which enabled them to withhold their support. Unprincipled politicians would have the perfect excuse for hoodwinking the electorate almost with impunity. This would break another link in the chain of democratic accountability between the representative and the local elector.

It would further weaken local influence. There is already disquiet amongst local party members when there are changes in government policies which break with agreed commitments of the party. Under PR, party leaders will be able to retort that since coalitions are a fact of life, compromising upon or abandoning party policies are necessary if they are ever to achieve office.

In government, this centralising process will be heightened. Party leaders will be able to claim, when answering criticism from their members, that policies unpopular to them had to be followed as part of a coalition deal. It will be hard to be sure whether or not that is the case, since by its very nature the business of agreeing coalitions is not an open one. Inevitably, it means wheeler-dealing behind closed doors and therefore a further concentration of power in the hands of political elites.

This was acknowledged by the political scientist Sartori, a proponent of an 'elitist' system of democracy. He argued quite unashamedly that PR would be a good thing because it invariably produces coalition governments which make it difficult for the electorate to 'pin down who is responsible' for decisions.[27] He was arguing against popular participation in politics and in favour of rule by elites which, although democratically elected by periodic votes, should not be subjected between elections to pressure from the populace below. Another political scientist has argued in similar terms that STV would encourage a 'moderate leadership' of the Labour Party because

35

it would 'help to protect the parliamentary party from extra-parliamentary control'.[28] In other words, it would undermine the accountability of political elites to local party members, community groups and trade unions.

Stability

Part of the case for such an elitist system of democracy is that, by being less vulnerable to fluctuations in popular opinion, it is supposed to encourage stability. This in turn is seen as an advantage for industry, facilitating forward planning and boosting economic confidence. In social terms, stability clearly provides for a more orderly society. But if stability has such virtues, it also contains the potential vice of being insensitive to the need for change – a tension which PR supporters do not appear to acknowledge.

They argue that one of the main benefits of PR is that it would, as Roy Jenkins put it in 1981, create 'greater stability of national direction and policy'.[29] This, it is maintained, contrasts with 'lurches' in policy, as the major parties succeed each other in office. But this picture can be exaggerated. For most of the post-war period up until 1979 there was a wide consensus whichever party held office: party rhetoric may have camouflaged this, but reality told a different story. That consensus started to fracture in the early 1970s because Britain's economic crisis deepened, rather than because of any inherent failing in the electoral system.

Economic pressures, international forces and class struggles have a much more significant impact on stability than electoral arrangements. Sometimes PR and stable government go hand in hand – as in West Germany since the War, for instance. Sometimes they do not – as in Germany before Hitler gained power or in Italy since the War.

Britain is commonly regarded as having an exceptionally stable society compared even with other industrially advanced countries in Europe. Yet few people put this down to the first-past-the-post system – though on similar assumptions to those of PR devotees, such a case could no doubt be made. Most would point to cultural, industrial, class and geographical factors as being those mainly responsible for Britain's relative stability. Similarly, widening class divisions, deepening poverty, increasing unemployment and racism would be seen as more important issues behind the social instability, urban riots and picket line conflicts of Britain in the 1980s than the absence of PR.

Even in its own terms, however, the claims that PR would bring greater stability are questionable. Italy's 'Imperiali' system of PR introduced in 1946 has in the last 40 years led to 46 different governments. Admittedly there has been some consistency of policy – mainly because of the domination of these governments by the Christian Democrats – but it is hardly a good advertisement for 'stable' or 'effective' government. Nor was the post-War Fourth Republic in France, where various PR arrangements resulted in 25 different governments and 15 prime ministers in just 13 years between 1945 and 1958.

Faced with this, a leading PR advocate, Enid Lakeman, conceded that there had indeed been intense instability in France. Pointing to the traditional problem of French politics – its many parties – she argued: 'The causes of the multiplicity of parties and instability of governments are too various and fundamental to be cured by a change in the electoral system alone.' She went on: 'In . . . Italy and France, it has been shown that the introduction of proportional representation was not responsible for the large number of parties and political instability; these conditions had already existed under the disgarded majority system.'[30]

But this turns the logic of the pro-PR case on its head. It is precisely the argument that PR supporters – Ms Lakeman included – normally prefer to deny, namely that the *political culture* of a given country is far more important than its exact *electoral* procedures. It is significant that the reality of the French and Italian experience forced her to support one of the very points being made in this book: that claims out of all proportion are made on behalf of PR.

Germany's Weimar Republic had 20 governments in 14 years under a List system. It also had hyper-inflation, mass unemployment, economic crises and dangerous political extremism. It is not suggested that these problems were caused by PR, but that they existed in spite of it. Some have argued that PR actually assisted Hitler's subsequent rise to power, partly because he initially had no real base at constituency level, partly because he gained a parliamentary foothold through the representation accorded under the German system of PR to splinter parties, and partly because he was able to exploit the opportunities opened up by a weak series of coalition governments. Others, pro- and anti-PR, contest this on the grounds that economic conditions were so serious that Hitler would have succeeded under any electoral system. But whether or not that is the case, the real issue is that PR did not *prevent* the rise of the Nazis: it did not block the most dangerous growth of extremism yet seen in Europe.

The rise of fascism in Italy also occurred under a PR system first introduced in 1919, and under which Mussolini came to power in 1922. The 1967 Colonel's coup in Greece happened despite PR arrangements first introduced in 1926 and subsequently modified. In other words, the record of PR over political stability has been less than impressive.

Small extreme-right groups have succeeded under PR, which they would not have done under first-past-the-post. In France the racist National Front won 35 seats in parliament and 135 regional councillors under the country's new List system in March 1986. With just under 10 per cent of the vote, it held the balance of power in parliament and in nine of the 26 regional councils. Under France's previous 'double ballot' voting system, the Front would not have had a single deputy (MP).

If STV, the preferred option of British PR supporters, had been introduced here, the National Front would certainly have gained seats in local government elections in the 1970s, and possibly in the 1979 general election too – enabling it to achieve the credibility and electoral breakthrough it needed to avoid its sharp decline after 1979. Under a Dutch-type List system, the NF would have won 3 parliamentary seats in 1979.

Anomalies

It is often pointed out that there can be indefensible anomalies under the first-past-the-post system. But PR is not immune from this affliction either.

Under the Additional Member system in Britain there could be extraordinary anomalies, even with a threshold vote such as in Germany (requiring a 5 per cent barrier to be overcome to secure MPs). As has been pointed out, it would be in the interests of the nationalist forces in Scotland, Wales and Northern Ireland to form a 'celtic alliance', contesting seats across the country (even in England) simply in order to build up their national vote. If, for example, 30 million people voted in a British general election, with the 'celtic alliance' winning 1,499,999 votes, it would probably get no seats. But, with the backing of just one extra voter (cast, say, in Bognor Regis), it would get over 30 seats.[31] This precise outcome is unlikely, but the very fact that the various nationalist groups have started discussing an electoral agreement shows that it is not quite as fanciful as might be supposed.

The complexities of List systems bring their own peculiarities. There are lengthy ballot papers (in Belgium's List system, 'a typical voting paper looks like the racing page of the sports edition of an evening paper,' concedes one PR enthusiast).[32] There are also complex counting procedures and calculations using elaborate formulae which may take several days. In the 1981 general election in Israel, held under the country's national List system, it took more than a week to finish all the counting and determine the final result.

Under the STV system used in the 1982 Northern Ireland Assembly elections, there were 26 names on ballot papers, and 23 separate counts were required to determine a result almost two days after counting began. In addition, it may often be far from clear to voters why one candidate has been elected and another not, especially under STV, where second, third and maybe even fourth or fifth preferences could determine an outcome itself produced by complex calculations.

Complexity is, of course, not in itself a strong argument against PR. Anomalies abound under first-past-the-post as

39

well. Computerisation could speed up and simplify counting. But these problems need to be considered in weighing the balance of the argument.

Majority rule?

An important argument for PR is that it does ensure that a government has the support of at least half the electorate, either by one party gaining an absolute majority of the votes on its own, or by a coalition of two or more parties doing so. Under the present system, by contrast, it is possible for either Labour or the Tories to win an overall majority of MPs with not much more than a third of the popular vote.

But on top of the questions posed earlier in this chapter about the disadvantages in terms of a loss of democratic accountability under PR – particularly the fact that the coalition government which emerges might not command majority support if the electorate were specifically invited to endorse it – there are other issues which need addressing.

A PR-elected coalition government may well 'represent' over half the voters at the moment it takes office. But since voters have not been able to endorse its programme, implementing its policies could be unpopular and its claims to be representative could melt away – in which case, another coalition more accurately reflecting majority public opinion at that time ought to be formed.

Post-War governments elected under the existing system with just under half the votes have experienced a decline in their popularity. In 1945 Labour won with 48 per cent, but opinion polls found its support frequently as low as 38 per cent. In 1955 the Conservatives won with just under 50 per cent, but reached a low of 34 per cent in 1958. In other words, governments elected with almost half the popular vote lost up to a third of their support in office.

More recently, with an increasingly volatile electorate, governments have experienced even more dramatic falls in their popularity. Within two years of winning with 48 per cent in 1966, Labour's standing in opinion polls fell to 26 per cent.

Elected on 44 per cent of the vote in 1979, the Tories dropped to 23 per cent in the polls in 1981. In 1983 the Tories won with 42 per cent, but polls early in 1986 showed their support down to as low as 27 per cent.

There is no reason why the same story should not unfold under coalition governments. For it is the *policies* which governments follow rather than the electoral system which is the crucial issue in determining the degree of popular consent they enjoy. As will be argued in the final chapter, it is far more important to introduce a new system of government that devolves the maximum possible power to ordinary voters so that they can influence policies in between elections, rather than to be pre-occupied with electoral arrangements which affect things only once every four or five years. It goes without saying that there is considerable merit in the argument that governments should win a majority of votes, but this should be placed in perspective. *Democratic accountability* rather than *electoral proportionality* is the key issue in determining what 'majority rule' actually means at any given time.

Local councillors

Equally strong criticisms can be directed at the introduction of PR in local government. Research has shown that most people identify a sense of community most strongly with their 'home area' or their 'neighbourhood', usually defined as no more than the size of a local council ward; nearly half see it in the even smaller terms of a polling district area or their immediately surrounding streets.[33]

Although we have more than one councillor representing wards under first-past-the-post, the multi-member councillor seats under STV would be much bigger – more like the size of present parliamentary seats. This would undermine any sense of neighbourhood representation. Given that councillors who are voluntary and have only minimal back-up facilities find it difficult as it is to keep in close touch with their wards, this would be even more true in wards on average five times the size of present ones. The same problems of accountability

41

would also apply, with the focus shifting away from the smallest political unit – the ward party branch and the ward community – towards branches the size of current constituency parties.

Power and class

The central question is not the one posed by PR supporters of being for or against the current electoral arrangements. It is what notion of democracy is being advocated. Opposition to the existing political system can be based upon support for a more participatory and accountable form of democracy, a genuine alternative to the system of minority class domination operated by centralised power elites which passes for democracy in Britain today.

Support for PR is not only associated with a conservative notion of democracy. Leading PR supporters favour a type of consensual politics which is artificial in that it does not reflect real divisions and conflicts in our society. One argued: 'Advocates of proportional representation wish to see adversary politics replaced by the politics of mutual accommodation.'[34] The problem is that 'adversary politics' in Britain is based upon the competing claims of different classes and groups which cannot be reconciled easily, if at all: one can only be advanced at the expense of the other. 'Accommodating' them means in practice leaving dominant groups still in control: it is *their* power structure designed to benefit their interests which subordinate groups would be 'accommodated' into as compliant partners in a new 'consensus'.

Liberal and SDP leaders constantly criticise the Labour and Tory parties for being 'class parties' and therefore unable to represent all the people; their own parties, by contrast, claim to stand above class divisions and represent 'the whole nation'. This is based upon a conservative analysis of the nature of power in contemporary Britain. It regards the articulation of class forces in the terms of pressure groups defending sectional interests, ignoring the fact that the class system is fundamental to determining the whole distribution of political, economic and social power. Advocating a politics based upon 'partnership' and 'harmony' between the classes does not face up to the reality of the dominant class remaining powerful regardless of which party (or which coalition) happens to be in office.

This dominance is felt throughout society, and particularly in the balance of economic power. The minority which forms the dominant class wields enormous economic power through its virtual monopoly of wealth. For instance, no more than 5 per cent of the population owns 96 per cent of all company stocks and shares.[35] Without altering this, 'partnership' between social classes becomes a device by which a minority can remain in the saddle, legitimating and reinforcing their power over the majority.

As even a strongly pro-PR academic had to concede when examining the history of electoral reform, the argument that PR would cut through class divisions does not stand up. Social and political developments have been dictated by 'the growth of more class based politics in Britain regardless of electoral mechanics,' he wrote.[36]

A diversion

Indeed one of the least convincing characteristics of the PR case is the fervour with which it is pressed as almost a panacea for all Britain's ills. In the more polemical PR tracts, it is advocated in terms which suggest that tiresome party wrangles and political extremism could be overcome almost at a stroke, leading to the emergence of a new dynamic politics. As a Liberal pamphlet typically put it:

> Proportional representation is likely to release a flood of incisive and radical intelligence into a government no longer enshrined by the shibboleths of class and party doctrine. It would also generate much-needed hope for our political institutions.[37]

PR is often peddled in an entirely escapist manner, as an illusory way out of the economic and political crisis which has steadily been closing in on Britain. When the SDP and the Liberals first launched their Alliance in Spring 1981, PR came top of the list on their joint political programme. The main thrust of the economic programme presented to the SDP's 1985 annual conference by the Party's economic spokesperson, Ian Wrigglesworth MP, was that the solution to Britain's economic problems depended upon electoral reform: 'PR is more important than the PSBR,' he said in a rhetorical flourish.[38] If he had meant that the PSBR (Public Sector Borrowing Requirement) should not be accorded the importance in policy making which the Thatcher government had given it, most people would agree. But the context of the remark was quite different, emphasising the absolutely key role of PR in a new approach, singularly devoid of hard economic policy, to overcoming Britain's economic crisis. In March 1986 the SDP Leader David Owen published a book, *A United Kingdom*, in which he argued that PR was the *main* agency for reversing Britain's economic decline and overcoming its social and class divisions.

The truth is that the precise nature of electoral arrangements counts for very little in achieving economic success. Provided the system is *democratic*, the exact features of its voting structure are unlikely to be as important to prosperity as the distribution of wealth and power, the structure of finance and industry and the level of investment.

Nor is it even obvious that PR would alter the basic structure of political power and government. As one political scientist who favours PR admitted:

> Electoral systems can, at best, provide greater scope for new patterns of behaviour amongst political actors; the routines of the past might in the end prove to be too deeply ingrained in the national culture to allow a change in the character of British government.[39]

There is no evidence to suggest that the ordinary citizen at an individual level or disadvantaged groups at a societal level will have their relationship to the centres of power altered at all by PR. The balance of *party* power could well change. But political power will remain concentrated in Britain's highly centralised system of government, and economic power will remain in the hands of the dominant class.

Main points against PR

Whilst PR would make for a fairer electoral system, its supporters have not shown how it would provide a more democratic system, for the reasons discussed earlier and now summarised.

First, vital links between local communities and their elected MPs or councillors would be undermined by both List and STV systems. The whole principle of democratic accountability would be weakened just when it needs strengthening.

Second, instead of emerging with a clear overall majority after an election, it is more probable that governments would only emerge after intense behind-the-scenes manoeuvring and bargaining. This might well produce government programmes bearing only a slight resemblance to the policies placed before the electorate by the parties concerned.

Third, far from invigorating British politics, it is possible that PR would breed further public disillusionment with party politics as real debate moved even further from the public to the private arena. More policy decisions would tend to be taken in secret deals, and governments could change hands without prior consultation with voters, as happened in West Germany in 1982 when the smaller Free Democrats abruptly switched from supporting the Social Democrats and went into coalition with the Christian Democrats.

Fourth, the tendency towards coalitions would give undue power to small, unrepresentative groups which would be able not only to make or break governments, but to extract policies to advance their sectional interests which had little support across the country. Meanwhile, much larger parties (probably of the left) could be excluded from power.

Fifth, the forces of the *status quo* would almost inevitably be strengthened and defended because the coalition process usually produces centrist governments. The politicians in them may change, but the general policy stance of these governments is less likely to. This is partly because inter-party bargaining over their respective policies tends to produce an outcome based upon the lowest common denominator around which agreement can be secured. Another reason is that the absence of single-party government, which has clear objectives and is

45

more clearly accountable, means that various ruling elites will have greater scope for exercising decisive influence. As will be shown in the next chapter, this is indeed one of PR's main attractions for sections of the City, the media and the Whitehall establishment. They see in PR an even more effective method than they have now for allowing them to retain effective power regardless of which particular party holds office.

Sixth, PR systems are not simply complex and confusing, they often provide no real connection between voters' first preferences – i.e. what they positively believe in – and the final results, which tend to reflect what they are least opposed to.

Seventh, by encouraging smaller parties and shifting government arrangements, PR would not increase political stability and may even decrease it in times of economic upheaval.

The case for first-past-the-post

By contrast, although the existing first-past-the-post system in Britain cannot claim to be as fair, it has a number of advantages over PR.

First, the single-member constituency provides for an obvious and *direct relationship* between the MP and his or her constituents. This relationship is very far from perfect in practice, but it is an important principle of British democracy. People know that the constituency in which they live is represented by one individual, to whom they can go with problems or whom they can seek to persuade. Most MPs hold regular advice surgeries for their constituents and can help to apply pressure on the local council. They are increasingly the focus for activity and pressure on local issues.

Second, there are clear lines of *local accountability*. The MP is selected by the local party and should remain accountable to it, enabling those active in local politics to have a direct input into the national political system. Similarly, the MP is answerable to the local community by facing periodic elections in which his or her record can be endorsed or rejected. Although most people vote on party lines, there is a 'local' element to voting in parliamentary elections which can be significant if an MP is either popular or unpopular locally.

Third, the candidate who receives the *largest number* of votes is the winner. Candidates cannot be elected as a result of second, third or fourth preferences, possibly beating those with more first preferences. There is a clear winner – the person whom most people positively want.

Fourth, it is a *straightforward* system which is easy to understand. The ballot paper is simple, there is a clear choice between alternative governments, and a direct connection between votes cast and the result at either constituency or national level. This is not to make the fatuous suggestion that British voters would somehow be less able to cope than their European counterparts with the complexities of STV ballot papers or the complicated counting systems which determine the outcome. The argument is rather that there are merits in a procedure under which the winner is unambiguous: the person who obtains most first preferences.

Fifth, there is a clear choice between the *political programmes* of rival parties. These programmes may be departed from in practice. But it is an important democratic principle that voters should be presented with clear policy choices. In the Labour Party's case, the programme put to the electorate is determined by a process of democratic discussion and decision-making which allows for considerable accountability, providing a link between party democracy and parliamentary democracy. The current system has the merit of giving people the right to choose between rival programmes, encouraging those programmes to be taken seriously, discouraging a form of politics revolving around personalities, and enabling voters to assess the extent to which the party in power has fulfilled its election promises.

Sixth, the electorate can vote for a *government* to carry through its policy. There is much more scope for individual votes to determine the character of governments than under the backroom wheeler-dealing virtually guaranteed by PR. There is also less likelihood of a stalemate, with no government being formed.

Seventh, there is less opportunity for *minority parties* to be

47

given power disproportionate to their support. Since major parties have a greater chance of forming a government on their own, minority groups are less likely to become as pivotal as is often the case under PR, where they can exert influence quite disproportionate to their popular support.

Eighth, although the present system can act in a conservative way by making it very difficult for newer forces and parties to achieve a breakthrough, there is little danger of the kind of *proliferation* of parties often experienced under PR, leading to constantly shifting coalitions. In the Netherlands, for instance, there was a marked proliferation after the introduction of PR in 1918. In the eight previous elections, no more than seven parties had been returned. But, immediately a List system was introduced, the number jumped to 17, and by 1967 there were as many as 27 parties represented in parliament. In 1981 ten parties gained representation in the Dutch Lower House, only one of which had gained as much as 30 per cent of the vote; the subsequent process of forming a government took 118 days – which then fell three weeks later. Although the introduction of PR in Germany and Ireland saw a reduction in the number of parties, PR is inherently more likely to sponsor party proliferation and shifting alliances.

Ninth, the system does permit *major changes* in direction and policy. A permanent centrist coalition wedded to the *status quo* is less likely, major parties of the left can come to power and radical changes can be implemented by winning a parliamentary majority.

It should be clear, therefore, that a judgement on the desirability of PR over first-past-the-post is more finely balanced than most PR advocates concede, and is ultimately a political question about democratic priorities rather than a moral question about fairness.

5

THE REALPOLITIK OF PR

A striking feature of the political stances adopted towards PR
is the extent to which they have been guided by calculations
of party advantage rather than basic arguments of principle.

Most parties in Britain have at different times supported
and opposed PR. Even the Liberal Party, its most consistent
and vociferous supporter, only adopted the idea in 1922 when
the party started to decline: just a few years before that the
Liberals had actually formed majority governments capable of
introducing PR.

The Labour Party supported electoral reform for a brief
period after the First World War when it was pessimistic about
the prospect of a breakthrough under the first-past-the-post
system; when that breakthrough came, Labour discarded its
policy.

During periods of Tory unpopularity significant numbers
of Conservatives have promoted PR as a way of stopping
Labour, only to draw back when the Tory Party recovered.
This was most noticeable in the early 1980s.

Minority groups like the Communist and Green parties have
seen PR as a mechanism for gaining a toehold in Parliament
which they would otherwise be denied. Some ultra-leftists have
seen it as a vehicle for splitting the Labour Party and achieving
a re-alignment of the left in which their own small groups
would be more prominent.

This is not to say that all those involved in the PR debate
lack integrity or have no genuine democratic concerns. But all
too often expediency has ruled the day in the politics of both
anti- and pro-PR positions.

Indeed, an examination of the *realpolitik* of PR gives a deeper insight into the democratic issues at stake. Although its supporters do not form a monolithic bloc (they come from left and right), the *dominant* momentum for PR contains a number of common themes: opportunism, centrism and support for capitalism.

Opportunism

The opportunist element is most clearly evident amongst leading Social Democrats. None of the SDP's founding 'Gang of Four' – Roy Jenkins, Bill Rodgers, David Owen and Shirley Williams – were at all enamoured of PR until they thought about leaving the Labour Party. Then they suddenly discovered its virtues.

Roy Jenkins was the first, when he floated the idea of a new 'Centre Party' in the BBC's prestigious Dimbleby Lecture in 1979. Bill Rodgers and David Owen expressed no interest in PR until they launched the SDP in 1981; indeed, both had opposed it over the years, notably during the 1972-4 period of Liberal revival and the 1977-8 Labour/Liberal pact.*

As recently as 24 November 1979, David Owen wrote to *The Times* in terms which contrast dramatically with his later conversion to a PR enthusiast. 'Proportional representation does not of itself guarantee political stability,' he argued. 'We should be very wary before we give up our system of coalition within parties and replace it with a system of coalition across parties.' In a book published in spring 1981 he repeated much the same argument,[40] although he also came out much more firmly in favour of electoral reform (on grounds of fairness) than he had before.[41] Subsequently, PR became one of his main campaigning issues as Leader of the SDP. For example, he devoted an entire Party Political Broadcast to the subject with comedian John Cleese in January 1986.

* They were, however, in the majority of the Labour Cabinet which in 1977 supported the principle of a regional List system for elections to the European Assembly.

By the time of the 1983 general election, Shirley Williams was a forceful advocate of PR. In 1970 she had turned down flat a strong academic case that PR might assist Catholics to get fair representation in the Northern Ireland parliament because she feared it might boost the Liberals' campaign for PR throughout Britain: 'What would Jeremy Thorpe [the Liberal Leader] make of it?', she responded.[42] She made no mention of PR in her book published in 1981, a wide-ranging review of most major policy areas and a virtual manifesto for the SDP.[43] The political journalist, Peter Kellner, takes up the story:

> I asked her why the book contained nothing about electoral reform. She replied that she did not mind one way or the other about proportional representation; in her view it was tosh to think that Britain's social and economic performance had anything to do with the particular electoral system the country enjoyed. 'But Roy, Bill and David were keen on PR, so I went along with them.'
>
> Two months later, Mrs Williams posed with David Steel for a launch of *A Fresh Start for Britain*, the statement of common principles shared by the SDP and the Liberals. This stated that 'the key' to social and economic progress 'lies in electoral and contitutional reform. We are committed to obtaining proportional representation at the earliest opportunity, because it is a pre-condition of the new politics which Britain needs.' Mrs Williams had either changed her mind dramatically, or was now putting her name to a view she privately felt to be bunkum. A few weeks later, on the BBC TV programme, *The Editors*, I argued that the press had been soft on divisions within the SDP leadership and, in Mrs Williams' presence, cited the difference of views over electoral reform. She immediately cut in to deny that any such difference existed.
>
> Afterwards, in the hospitality room, I invited Mrs Williams to elaborate on her denial, in the light of what she told me a few months earlier. Yes, she replied, she remained unconvinced by the claims made for PR, but she was not actually opposed to electoral reform. That was why she had given such a firm denial on the air.
>
> Happy with that reply, she smiled attractively and disappeared into the night.[44]

Of course, people are entitled to change their views, and it is also quite legitimate to feel more strongly about some party policies than others. Nonetheless, the sudden and somewhat ambiguous conversion of SDP leaders underlines the role of self-interest in the PR cause.

A middle way

PR is inextricably bound up with the role which the SDP and Liberals seek to perform: a centrist force between what they call the 'extremes' of Labour and the Tories.

Apart from its objective of creating a fairer electoral system, PR is also seen as a vehicle for a different type of politics. Its advocates argue that Britain has been plagued by 'adversary politics'. By this they mean 'the maintenance of relationships of political competition through a mode of argument which assumes that political questions can best be resolved if expressed in terms of two and only two contrasting alternatives. Since by a happy coincidence it is held that such alternatives are usually voiced by alternative groups of politicians, adversary politics becomes more than a way of conducting political argument: it becomes a mechanism of choice too.'[45]

The traditional two-party system which has tended to predominate in Britain under first-past-the-post is seen as having created a particularly debilitating form of adversary politics. It is suggested that political decisions are made to conform to the self-interest of the class and ideological blocs which each of the major two parties has represented, and that this has meant a de-stabilising oscillation of policies back and forth according to whether Labour or the Tories were in power.

This grossly exaggerates the extent to which post-War British governments have pursued radically different policies and seriously underestimates the extent of the consensus between them – at least until the Thatcherites broke from it in 1979. However, the argument is that decisions should be made in a consensual way, by drawing together different views to find common points of agreement. It is believed that decisions arrived at in this way would be of a much better quality than those reached through the adversarial process of inter-party competition. To support this, it is further argued that the adversarial system of British politics has been at the heart of the country's social, economic and political decline.[46] Leaving aside the highly dubious basis for this assertion (which is wholly unproven), a new consensual process of decision-making is not simply advanced to secure decisions that are 'better' in some technical or neutral way. The assumption made is that 'good' decisions are 'moderate' or 'middle way' ones. And here the crucial role of PR is evident.

As a leading protagonist writes: 'The debate over abandoning this [first-past-the-post] system for one of proportional representation is in effect a debate over hastening the demise of the two-party system and hence over the practicability and desirability of moving to coalition-style government.'[47] He adds that a 'considerable' advantage of changing to PR 'would be greater moderation in policy . . . since the system would become more a multiparty one than at present and it is unlikely that a party would obtain an absolute majority of seats in the House, each of the major parties, if it wanted to form a government, would have to cooperate with a party or parties taking a more central political stance.'[48]

PR and the centre-right

Another motivation behind PR is even more ideological. It includes two related objectives. On the one hand, PR is promoted as a means of stopping a socialist – or, to be more specific, a left Labour – government from achieving office. On the other, it is seen as a mechanism for securing a centre-right coalition which could govern Britain permanently. These arguments make no mention of 'fairness' or 'greater democracy': such slogans are directed at public opinion, while the real agenda behind PR remains hidden.

In 1958 sections of the Conservative Party were concerned that the rise in Liberal support might split the 'anti-socialist vote', and they argued for electoral reform by the Alternative Vote which, though not fully proportional, could prevent this split from occurring. The *Economist* magazine also recommended this as 'a mechanism by which the Tory-preferring middle vote would not be "wasted" . . . and an assurance that thumping Labour majorities in the House of Commons will not again be built on a minority Labour vote in the country'.[49]

Similar concerns resurfaced in the 1970s and 1980s amongst a minority in the Conservative Party. Their motive – and they have been perfectly open about it – sprang from an anxiety about the long-term decline of the Tory vote (from 50% in 1955 to as low as 36 per cent in October 1974 and then 42 per cent in 1983).[50] Standing in the Disraeli/Macmillan tradition of pragmatic (or 'wet') Toryism which believes that whichever party holds office, conservatism should rule, their support for PR dated almost exactly from the leftward swing of the Labour Party in the early 1970s.

They set up a ginger group, 'Conservative Action for Electoral Reform', and two of its leading MPs, Sir Nigel Fisher and Tim Rathbone, argued:

We believe that the Conservative Party would thrive if proportional representation was introduced, because we are the most loyal party, with the largest traditional following, the best organised and probably the best financed. Given PR, we could confidently expect to dominate a right of centre coalition for many years.[51]

In a joint comment on the 1981 Warrington by-election (which Labour held against a strong SDP performance, with the Tories deeply unpopular), the two MPs made it clear that their objective was to stop socialism. Concerned at the poor showing of the Tory candidate and the relatively good result for the SDP, they argued:

the one thing which so many of the voters of Warrington voted *for* was SDP commitment to the introduction of more proportionate elections to the House of Commons which would then protect them from the extremes of socialism . . . The potential to commit, measured by every single opinion poll recently, and the readiness to commit as shown by votes for the SDP in this by-election, has even greater importance for the Conservative Party than the SDP. Because if we wish generally to preserve from future socialist reversal the radical and long overdue

54

changes in our economy and our society which our Conservative Government has set itself to achieve, then it is imperative that our method of electing future governments must be changed to reflect more closely the essential good sense of the British electorate.[52]

Another Conservative underlined the argument in 1984. Writing just a year after the Tory general election landslide, he was nevertheless concerned about the election of a future Labour government:

there is an inherent likelihood that PR would produce a succession of coalitions, predominantly of a moderate, conservative character. This position would guarantee to the Conservatives what they essentially require; the continuance of the present economic and social system, judiciously reformed from time to time . . . a coalition between the Alliance and Conservatives . . . would give the sort of government which most Englishmen and women want . . . this . . . is what stands between the country and the risk of a Labour administration.[53]

That the British establishment was thinking in similar terms was indicated by *The Times*. Worried about the poor showing of Mrs Thatcher's government in late 1979, an editorial in the paper pointed to the danger of a Labour Government being elected and went on:

The obvious way to remove this danger is to change to a system of proportional representation. If Britain had any of the normal forms of proportional representation, there would be no danger of Marxist government being formed because there is absolutely no danger of a Marxist majority. They cannot get to 50 per cent. We should therefore be safe from the most damaging political event that could at present happen to us.[54]

Lest it be thought that the term 'Marxist' was referring to something more fanciful, the context left no doubt that it was referring to the possibility of a left Labour government elected, as most modern British governments have been, on a minority vote. An even blunter version of the same argument appeared in a leaflet published by Conservative Action for Electoral Reform: 'The present electoral system could easily give power to a Socialist Party controlled by an extreme left-wing group

. . . The Conservative Party will be taking an unjustified risk if we do not reform the Constitution . . . We have the power to extinguish the possibility of extreme left-wing government indefinitely. . .'[55] Again, for 'extreme left wing' read 'Labour'.

PR and capitalism

This shift to backing PR amongst sections of the dominant class in Britain was not based upon any desire to extend democracy; that may or may not have been a by-product, but it was certainly not the motive. The shift occurred, on the whole, after the early 1970s, in direct response to the collapse of several of the foundation stones of the British political system.

First of all, Labour moved significantly to the left after the 1970 election, when its defeat was widely seen within the party as a policy failure of Labour's right. In 1972 and 1973 Labour adopted radical policies for economic intervention, restructuring, and public ownership. When these policies were not pursued by the 1974-9 Labour administrations, there was further pressure to shift the party to the left, culminating in the democratic reforms of 1980-81 to increase leadership accountability, both through mandatory re-selection of MPs and the direct election of the Party Leader by an electoral college. It is of interest that the clamour for PR rose markedly at precisely these periods of left advance in 1972-3 and 1979-81.

Second, the rise of the new right in the Conservative Party after Margaret Thatcher's election as Leader in 1975 meant that the Tories jettisoned the politics of consensus which had existed in the post-War era. This was not welcomed by all elements in the dominant class in Britain, many of whom quickly became alarmed at the manner in which Thatcherism accelerated Britain's *industrial* decline, even if others welcomed the boost it gave to *finance* capital; there was also considerable anxiety that rapidly rising unemployment coupled with the stridency of the Thatcher Government's right-wing policies could provoke a reaction in favour of the left.

Third, the general breakdown during the 1970s of the post-War consensus inevitably had an impact on the pattern of politics. Fundamental to this breakdown was the end of the acceptance by both Labour and Tories of Keynesian methods of economic management and an expanding welfare state to ensure full employment and economic growth. More perceptive figures in the British establishment and business circles understood that the resulting polarisation was rapidly undermining the 'moderate' and consensus-based politics of traditional Labourism and Toryism. They feared that neither Party would be able any more to maintain social stability and the continuing expansion of capitalism.

Consequently, they sought to fashion a new consensus favourable to stability and to the accumulation of private capital. PR was seen as playing a key part in moulding the political dimension to such a new consensus. It offered the attraction of a permanent centre government, whichever parties were involved. It was also considered to hold out a greater prospect for policy continuity. As Conservative Action for Electoral Reform stated: 'The two-party system with each party in turn repealing the legislation of their opponents is bad for Britain and bad for Conservative interest. A free market economy cannot function without continuity of policy.'[56] A sister leaflet from the Tory group entitled 'Industry Needs Electoral Reform' argued that the adoption of PR 'is essential if we wish to create a more stable political environment in which industry can flourish'. The author, Viscount Caldecote, a top businessman, was at the time Chairman of Delta Metal Company. In a separate appeal, six top businessmen* made it quite clear that PR was necessary for 'business as usual':

> We are convinced that a major factor . . . would be the reform of our electoral system by introducing a system of proportional representation for parliamentary and other elections.
>   The great disadvantage of the present electoral system from the industrial point of view is that it frequently produces drastic and exaggerated changes in policy at intervals which are far

* Viscount Caldecote (Chairman, Delta Metal Ltd); Lord Carr (Chairman, Prudential Assurance); Sir Alex Jarratt (Chairman, Reed International); Joseph Rank (Chairman, Rank Hovis McDougall); Sir Leslie Smith (Chairman, BOC International); Sir Graham Wilkins (Chairman, Beecham Group Ltd).

too short to enable industry to plan and operate efficiently. There is a basic mismatch between the long lead times necessary for investment and development in complex modern industry and the 180 degree reversals of policy which occur at relatively short intervals not only as between, but also within, successive administrations.

Too often these changes owe far more to political dogma than to careful assessment of the national welfare, and are often supported by a minority of the electorate only. Moreover these policy shifts are usually unrelated to technological and market factors which determine the success of industry in creating real wealth and the prosperity of the whole community.[57]

Not surprisingly, business has been willing to fund the drive for PR. Barclays Bank, for instance, has financed the National Committee for Electoral Reform. Beechams and Hill Samuel supported the Alliance-dominated 'Campaign for Fair Votes' launched in January 1984. In 1981-2 the National Westminster Bank sponsored a series of sixth-form conferences organised by the Hansard Society, with school students taking part in mock elections using first-past-the-post and PR systems. (The Hansard Society had published its own study favouring PR in 1976.) Industrialists and financiers have been active in other ways on behalf of the PR lobby. In March 1981, for example, a body calling itself the 'City Committee for Electoral Reform' organised a banquet in the Guildhall presided over by Lord Carr, former Tory Cabinet Minister and Chairman of Prudential Assurance.

Shortly after the 1983 general election, a group of 10 leading industrialists – described as 'mainly enlightened Conservatives' – published a pamphlet stressing the 'instability' of the two-party system which, they maintained, was 'bad for business'.[58] New names joining those already identified with the PR lobby included Sir Richard Cave, Chairman of Thorn EMI, Sir Adrian Cadbury, Chairman of Cadbury-Schweppes, Lord Jellicoe, former Tory Cabinet Minister and Chairman of Tate & Lyle, and Sir Maurice Laing, Chairman of the Laing group.

In March 1985, the Confederation of British Industry published a booklet entitled *Change to Succeed*, proposing a new business strategy for economic prosperity based upon private enterprise. Apart from a programme of economic measures, it also favoured far-reaching constitutional changes, including more power for the House of Lords, a lengthening of the five-year parliamentary term, a more formal consultative relationship between government and business – and proportional representation. PR, the CBI felt, would help to overcome divisions in British society and create better conditions for business to prosper.

The other side of industry's advocacy of PR is a desire to control trade unions. Repeatedly in PR literature there is reference to the need to break 'divisive' union power. Whether or not PR would in practice wield such extraordinary influence is dubious – but its supporters *believe* it would. For example, a Liberal pamphlet stated that electoral reform would make it less easy for the TUC 'to bully the entire nation through the vehicle of a political party which is in their pocket'.[59] An SDP sympathiser, the leading political columnist Peter Jenkins, put the argument succinctly in 1981:

> Electoral reform would make it easier for governments to tackle the trade union problem with authority and continuity. Proportional representation at local government level would help to break the stranglehold which public employees are beginning to exercise over public services.[60]

Re-alignment

Underlying the *realpolitik* of PR is the yearning for a re-alignment of British politics. In December 1979 – after Roy Jenkins had first proposed a new centre party, but well before the Labour defections to the SDP – one of Britain's top financiers, Sir James Goldsmith, argued through the medium of an editorial in his magazine *Now!* that: 'Abandoning the first-past-the-post voting system is central to any successful re-alignment of political forces.'[61]

In 1981 Peter Jenkins clarified the argument in the *Guardian* when he wrote:

> one effect of a [left] . . . capture of the Labour Party would

be a significant increase in support for proportional representation on both the right-wing of the Labour Party and the left-wing of the Conservative Party . . . important for the future would be the existence of a substantial group within the Labour Party, in effect a party within a party, which would be prepared to block the implementation of certain . . . [left] policies or, perhaps, even coalesce with centre-left elements capable of forming an acceptable majority or preventing the formation of an unacceptable one.[62]

Since this was written *after* the formation of the SDP, Jenkins was talking about those in the Labour Party who had remained loyal members. To that extent, the launch of the SDP was viewed as just the first stage in a wholesale political re-alignment, to be completed by the introduction of PR. For one of the arguments deployed by PR protagonists is that the traditional parties are in themselves coalitions, containing a range of opinions. In the short term, PR, they say, would enable such 'submerged' coalitions to become 'open' ones.[63] In the longer term, because PR encourages a multiplicity of parties, the right and left wings of the Labour Party would sever their link and form different groups, the right making a pact with the Alliance which would ideally lead to the emergence of a stronger centre party.

The fact that PR is also supported by elements on the left – albeit for different reasons, as will be evident in the next chapter – should not obscure the nature of the main ideological momentum behind it: a momentum which has little to do with improving democracy and everything to do with cementing a new centre-right consensus to follow the era of Thatcherism.

6

THE LEFT AND ELECTORAL REFORM

Support for proportional representation has produced some unlikely bedfellows. When the Labour Campaign for Electoral Reform was launched in November 1979, its Chairman was Tom Ellis MP (soon to be a defector to the SDP) and its most prominent sponsor was Arthur Scargill. The Communist Party has long backed electoral reform and well-known figures on the left have favoured PR – amongst them Ken Livingstone, Tariq Ali and Robin Blackburn.

However, these left-wingers have not normally advocated any one PR option: the case is invariably put in the most general terms, often in ignorance of the full implications of either STV or List systems. It is therefore important to assess the arguments socialists have advanced in support of PR to establish whether these overcome the many objections to it.

Labour party backers

PR first attracted support from the left a long time ago. Before the First World War, many in the Labour Party feared they would not succeed under the first-past-the-post system, with its bias against third parties. Indeed, such was the interest in PR that had the Labour Leader Ramsay MacDonald not been so vehemently opposed – he believed it would make the House of Commons less representative – the Party could well have included it as a commitment in election manifestos.[64]

In January 1913, Philip Snowden MP (later to become a Labour Chancellor) wrote a pamphlet entitled *PR from a Labour Standpoint*, in which he stressed the electoral advantages to Labour if it adopted PR:

> It is incomprehensible that a Labour Party which is fighting its way to political representation in the face of tremendous difficulties can ignore the enormous help which such a reform as this would be . . . if a system of proportional representation was in operation at the next General Election, the Labour Party would certainly secure 110 Labour Members.[65]

For similarly self-interested reasons, many Labour MPs supported it until the 1920s. In 1918 the party conference actually came out in favour and in February 1923 a Bill to establish PR in local government elections received the backing of 74 Labour MPs (including Clement Attlee), with only 11 voting against. But as Labour's strength grew, support for PR receded. Whilst Labour MPs had supported the 1921 PR Bill by 25 to 5, they opposed the 1924 PR Bill by 90 to 28, and in 1926 the annual conference carried by a large majority a motion condemning it. The same conference did, however, leave open the possibility of backing the 'Alternative Vote' (AV) system. When a Bill favouring the AV was introduced in the Commons in 1931, it was actually carried by 295 (of whom 253 were Labour) to 230 (of whom 227 were Tories); the Bill eventually lapsed after becoming snarled up in the House of Lords.

More recent Labour support for PR has been less expedient, although the Labour Study Group on Electoral Reform (formed in 1976) did argue in a pamphlet that PR could stop Labour being pushed into permanent opposition.[66] The Labour Campaign for Electoral Reform (which absorbed the Study Group) emphasised an argument used by other left-wing advocates of PR: it would be 'undemocratic' to try to construct such a radically different system as socialism with less than half the vote, albeit with more than half the seats in the Commons. Elected on a minority vote, Labour would not have persuaded the country about the merits of socialism. Referring to the Labour governments of 1964 to 1979, the Labour Campaign stated that there was no point in trying to introduce 'radical, progressive reforms' when 'a democratic majority in the country did not understand and support us'.[67]

On the face of it, this is a fair argument: all *democratic* socialists know they must win majority support. But it is based upon a number of questionable assumptions. First of all, it is a rather crude model of political reality: obligatory opposition until the magic 50 per cent hurdle is cleared and socialism suddenly acquires legitimacy. It is absurd to suggest that socialism would be out of order with 49.9 per cent of the vote but given the green light at 50.1 per cent.

Much more realistic and no less democratic is a strategy which recognises that building true majority support for socialism will require not only persuading the mass of people when out of office, but also periods of Labour governments (elected under the existing system) which carry people with them towards socialist objectives. The aim would be to utilise a series of 'minority vote' (though 'majority MP') Labour governments to consolidate support for Labour policies, build new alliances with groups outside the labour movement and create a climate out of which a socialist society could be built.

Democratic socialism can never be imposed on an unwilling electorate and still remain democratic: it can only be introduced by a painstaking process of winning popular support. Nor can it conceivably be introduced in a short period: the fundamental changes needed to abolish capitalism and achieve a socialist transformation will take a long time.

The Labour Campaign for Electoral Reform also argues that PR would prevent local Labour parties in areas of solid Tory or Alliance support from 'dying on their feet'. But on that argument Labour would never have achieved the breakthrough it did in the 1920s. Additionally, until as recently as the late 1970s, many local Liberal parties had battled on for decades without the slightest prospect of winning – until their perseverance paid off and, especially in those areas where Liberals adopted a 'community politics' approach, they started to make gains. There are no short cuts to winning political support.

Another Labour advocate of PR repeats an argument found in pro-PR groups of all parties: the STV system would allow

Labour voters to determine the sort of Labour candidate they favoured, thereby eliminating from the party the debilitating divisions it experienced in the 1970s and early 1980s.[68] But it is unrealistic to imagine that the local Labour parties would choose a range of candidates across the left-right spectrum: they are far more likely to select candidates most in tune with their approach, and quite understandably so. The Hansard Society Report disputed the claim that such a choice would in practice be offered to the electorate, pointing out that under Ireland's STV system 'there is no conscious attempt to produce a slate of candidates across the political spectrum within a party and the emphasis is upon the personal/local links of the candidate'.[69]

One Labour left-winger who has favoured a specific PR option is Ken Livingstone, leader of the Greater London Council from 1981 to 1986. He argued in 1984:

> In principle I have always been in favour of proportional representation. By this I mean something like the German system, where over half the Members of Parliament are directly elected, and a topping-up then operates on the basis of the actual votes received by different parties. I would simply insist that the topping-up would have to be of defeated candidates, on the basis of the highest vote downwards. Otherwise you give too much power to the party bureaucracy.[70]

This is much the same as the Additional Member system favoured by the Hansard Society and suffers from the same defects, especially that of having two classes of MP and larger constituencies. However, Ken Livingstone did at least have a clear idea of what he meant by PR, which is rare among its left-wing backers.

Others on the left

Some left-wingers outside the Labour Party look forward to a final break in the left-right coalition which makes up the party, and the emergence of a 'purer' socialist party. This outcome, they argue, would both be encouraged by PR and would need PR if the left was to retain any foothold in the conventional party system. In truth, whether or not a re-alignment of the left is desirable – and in practice most previously independent socialists have joined Labour since the mid-1970s – to advocate splitting Labour would be to confine the left to an entirely marginal role in Britain for a very long time ahead. No doubt it is possible to imagine conditions in Britain in which socialism was so dominant that the left could afford the luxury of splitting and re-grouping. But for the foreseeable future, socialist forces will be struggling to achieve significant, let alone dominant, support and it would be pure self-indulgence to jeopardise that task by sacrificing the Labour Party on the altar of some vague re-alignment project which utilised PR.

A more credible argument has been advanced by those sympathetic to Labour but outside the party's mainstream. Labour's poor showing in 1983, coupled with demographic changes and the long-term decline in the party's vote since 1951, prompted one socialist academic, Michael Rustin, to argue:

> The most probable outcome of electoral contests under the existing rules seems to be a successful divide-and-rule operation by the Conservatives. So long as two Opposition parties or groupings divide the non-Conservative vote, Tories can continue to win elections on several per cent *less* of the vote than they secured in June 1983. This pattern in 1983 worked against the Labour Party more strongly than the Alliance, since Labour voters proved more willing to vote 'tactically' for the most strongly placed non-Tory candidate . . . The effect of such a destructive competition between Labour and the Alliance parties could be a long-term shift in the balance of political and class power in favour of the Right. . .[71]

Rustin sees PR as a method for securing a 'de facto truce' between Labour and the Alliance, instead of what he sees as 'the present war-to-the-death'.[72] As he makes clear, this would be part of constructing the 'anti-Thatcher alliance' which he (in common with the majority of the Communist Party) sees as offering the best hope for socialist forces.

Such a strategy is highly contentious on the left and also based on a misconception of the ideological objectives of the Alliance parties, who define their politics not in anti-Tory terms but in the much more realistic ones of *replacing* the Labour Party as the main opposition to the Tories. The SDP in particular sees itself operating as a moderating force *within* a Thatcherite consensus favouring market forces, private capital and an Atlanticist, pro-nuclear foreign and defence policy; in practice, the Liberals have gone along with this. How an anti-Thatcher alliance could be constructed except at the expense of virtually all Labour's distinctive, radical policies is not explained. It is also important to note that the *democratic* case for PR figures much less strongly in Rustin's argument than the *tactical* one.

Significantly, Rustin pays only the most cursory attention to the implications of implementing PR, conceding that there are 'technical issues to be considered', but regarding these as 'secondary'.[73] In reality, they are crucial: as this book makes clear, it is only by peering beneath the rhetoric of PR down to its practicalities that its many deficiencies can be identified. By and large the pro-PR left does not even show an awareness of the different PR options, let alone their advantages and disadvantages.

The British Communist Party (CP) has long backed electoral reform, specifically the STV system. In February 1944 the Communist MP for West Fife, Willie Gallacher, proposed to a Speaker's Conference that STV be introduced in parliamentary and local elections. Although self-interest may have been one reason for this, the CP's pro-PR position is consistent with the party's overall political strategy. Rather than repeating the arguments against STV, it is therefore necessary to assess Communist support for PR against a different yardstick.

Alliances for change

In the early 1980s, leading Communists argued that the 'key strategic problem now facing socialists is how to build a political majority that includes part of the centre but is under the leadership of the Left . . . a more flexible PR system will face Labour up to the need to build more deep rooted support . . .'[74] In keeping with this is their strategy of building 'alliances' for change. They believe that no one political party could hope to represent all the interests favouring political change in a progressive or leftward direction. These interests will only be advanced through the dynamic of different community, sectional, single-issue, trade union and political groups working together on specific questions where they have a common purpose.

The necessity for the left to strengthen and broaden its base of support is well taken – far too many socialists have been content with advancing by capturing positions within institutions rather than building popular, mass support for socialism. But to argue that PR would encourage such a 'mass' orientation requires a logical leap of faith: if the left needs to create new sources of support, it needs to do so regardless of the precise electoral arrangements within which it finds itself working. It is equally plausible to conclude that PR would *discourage* such a task, since the result would be a more fragmented left in which each group became preoccupied with building its own support. This is especially likely since the main organ of working-class representation, the Labour Party, would almost certainly be injured by the introduction of PR and thus cease to act as a unifying focus for socialist activity and pressure.

The Communists' rejoinder to that argument is to assert that PR would 'give a new energy to a whole range of minority political parties and democratic movements by increasing their chances of council and even parliamentary representation'.[75] They maintain that PR would allow alliances of feminists, greens, blacks, peace organisations and community groups to be given political representation. This is an argument echoed by radical Liberals. But, again, there is no evidence that this would occur.

The PR systems most widely favoured would all have a 'threshold' vote which parties would have to pass in order to secure representation. It is quite conceivable that under a List system this figure would be exceeded by minority parties (in Germany, with its 5 per cent threshold, the 'Greens' have been successful in doing so). But List systems are specifically rejected by Communists, radical Liberals and British Greens.

They all favour STV, which would require successful candidates in the five-member average seats to achieve a minimum of 17 per cent of the vote. This 17 per cent is the effective threshold. Even after preferences had been redistributed from the major parties, it is highly unlikely that minority forces would secure any representation at all. For a minority group to win the 17 per cent needed in a five member seat would leave just 83 per cent of the vote to be distributed between the three large parties. This may continue to happen in Scotland and Wales, where nationalist candidates have already won seats under first-past-the-post. In the very few inner-city areas with concentrations of black voters, a breakthrough might conceivably be achieved. But unless political conditions in Britain alter in an almost revolutionary way, Labour, the Tories and the Alliance will between them mop up all the MPs in constituencies averaging five members or less; only in the few city seats with more than five members would minority groups stand much chance.

STV could actually assist the *larger* parties. Much greater resources would be needed to fight the monster constituencies. Sustaining party structures and financing the necessary publicity and organisation needed in election campaigns will favour parties with the most resources. In a television age, where voters tend to form their opinions according to national media coverage, it requires considerable effort to achieve a breakthrough by local activity. This is even more the case during the election period, when voters are deluged with material from the main parties and treated to a daily torrent of political news in the media. For many decades it was difficult for the Liberals to contest the majority of single-member seats across the country because of inadequate resources. To suggest that much smaller groups could manage to make the necessary impact in seats five times the size is simply not credible.

Women

Another part of the left case is that PR would assist groups who have suffered severe under-representation under the current system, notably women and black people. In 1983 women formed 52 per cent of the electorate and just 3.5 per cent of MPs: 23 out of 650. In the twelve general elections since the War, the proportion of women MPs has averaged 3.7 per cent. It was at its highest (4.6 per cent) in 1964 and its lowest (3 per cent) in 1979. Furthermore, only 15 to 20 per cent of local councillors are women.[76]

Pressure for PR has come from some feminists rightly demanding that male dominance of Parliament and party power structures should give way to equality for women. Like many other arguments for PR, theirs has an initial plausibility to it. In principle, PR could be harnessed on behalf of *women* just as it could be on behalf of *parties*, and there is some evidence to suggest that this happens.

From the accompanying table, it does appear that PR produces better representation of women when it operates through List systems. Although it is difficult to generalize from just two examples, the difference under STV is marginal. However, the fact that countries with similar List systems produce such markedly different outcomes does confirm the importance of influences other than electoral procedures. No doubt the fact that List systems differ in their details could be a factor – but not one anything like important enough to explain, for example, why Finland has four times greater a representation of women than Israel. Political culture, the strength of feminist ideas and social attitudes as well as economic circumstances all play their part, and the exact role of the electoral system is not obvious.

The fact that Scandanavian countries with PR have more women MPs is probably due to the fact that feminist ideas and demands for equality are stronger in Scandanavia; this would probably have resulted in more women MPs under a first-past-the-post system as well. The Italian PR system, for instance, has not benefited women precisely because the dominant culture there obstructs women's emancipation. How

Electoral System	Women representatives as % of total
Single-member constituencies	
Britain (1983)	3.5
USA (1978)	3.7
New Zealand (1980)	4.3
Canada (1980)	5.0
STV	
Malta (1981)	4.6
Ireland (November 1982)	8.4
List systems	
Israel (1981)	6.6
Belgium (1978)	7.5
Portugal (1981)	7.5
Italy (1977)	8.4
Germany (1983)	9.8
Austria (1981)	10.0
Switzerland (1981)	10.5
Netherlands (1977)	15.3
Norway (1977)	22.5
Sweden (1981)	22.6
Denmark (1979)	23.4
Finland (1979)	26.0

Source: Vernon Bogdanor, *What is Proportional Representation?* (Martin Robertson, 1984), p. 114.

else is it possible to explain why Scandanavian legislatures contain over 20 per cent of women whereas in Italy the proportion is only 8 per cent, when both countries have List systems?

On the other hand, analysis of the German system tends to support the view that the List can assist women. In Germany a directly elected single-member procedure is complemented by topping up from party lists. Comparison of the two elements in voting for the German Bundestag shows that the number of women directly elected from constituencies is significantly less than those elected from Party lists.[77] This would seem to show that the opportunity afforded to parties to take positive action in composing their lists of candidates works to the advantage of women – though it may also be that since the 'topping up' element is the secondary one, women find themselves allocated to it rather than put forward as primary candidates in the constituency-based elections.

If a List system were to be adopted, there could be pressure on parties to allocate, say, half the places on the list to women. The Dutch Labour Party was persuaded to ensure that at least 25 per cent of its candidates are women. In Sweden, there has been pressure to achieve equal representation in both the Social Democratic and Liberal parties by ensuring that women and men candidates were on alternate positions on the lists. [78]

Clearly, that would dramatically advance the the position of women in politics. But would this justify agreeing to a List system which has all the deficiencies identified in Chapters Three and Four? Can the position of women be advanced only at the expense of undermining other fundamental democratic principles? Any advance made by securing a fairer deal for women in the short term would be negated by the longer-term damage which the List system would do to democratic participation and accountability. It is also significant that none of the strongest voices for PR – the Alliance, the Communists and the Greens – backs a List system.

They are thus in something of a quandry because, under their favoured STV system, there is no guarantee that women would do much better than under the present system. In multi-member constituencies, the selecting body would be an area-rather than a constituency-based party and it would be subject to exactly the same political forces which block the selection of women now. Arguably, those forces would be even greater, for the evidence suggests that women's participation in party activity is greatest at ward level and tails off at constituency or executive level where the style, timing and venue of meetings

71

have been traditionally tailored to men's behaviour and interests. This may be offset by the ability of feminists involved in their party's selection process not to use up all their allocation of votes and to support women only. By this method they could tip the balance in favour of women. But the main barrier against the advance of women is the lack of women participating in the selection process itself, which has nothing directly to do with the electoral system.

A massive change in social and political consciousness will be necessary to win equality for women in Parliament and the town halls. It is naive to imagine that PR alone could 'do the job' without such a fundamental change. To the extent that PR would concentrate power even more in the party machines, it would encourage a form of politics which feminists have opposed particularly strongly. A much more productive route is to press ahead with demands, such as those made within the Labour Party, for constitutional changes and equal rights to secure justice for women in all parties.

Black people

In 1983 there were no black MPs, even though black people formed 4.5 per cent of the national electorate and in some inner-city, single-member constituencies (in London and Birmingham, for instance) over 40 per cent.

Similar issues arise for black people as for women when assessing how PR would affect them. However, STV may be of more assistance in this case because the black community is concentrated into a relatively few urban areas of Britain. In such areas blacks could use their influence as voting blocs to insist on at least one black candidate standing in multi-member constituencies. On the other hand, as recent selections of more black candidates within the Labour Party have shown, blacks can advance under first-past-the-post too.

It is sometimes argued that PR would enable black people to vote *en bloc* to secure black councillors or MPs. One leading Communist has argued that such a move should be encouraged, because achieving proper representation for the black community is such an urgent necessity that 'many people feel it overrides "party" political considerations.'[79]

But this leads us into deep water. Is the argument that we need to move towards a system of 'functional' representation of political interests? This would be a system where competing groups with particular interests or functions vote for their own representatives – women for women MPs, blacks for black MPs, maybe those in education voting for 'educational' MPs, pensioners for 'elderly MPs', and so on. This would short-circuit the idea of 'general' representation, which seeks to aggregate various interests under a common programme where political priorities can be ordered coherently in relation to each other, rather than left to the vagaries of interest-group bargaining and special pleading. The implicit idea that, say, working-class blacks would benefit from a black representative regardless of his or her class and political background is also dubious.

Autonomous organisation of black people is an important principle which needs to be defended. Self-organisation can pressure the conventional political structures into recognising black oppression and black aspirations. Establishing black sections within the major parties can also assist with this process. But to extend this into an argument for separate black political *parties* (which is effectively what is being suggested) would confine black politics to a ghetto existence and for that very reason is most unlikely to be endorsed by the black community. Even in the USA, where the party system is much weaker and where politics is based much more on interest-groups, that has not happened.

Greater equality?

In short, it is by no means proven that PR would encourage the greater equality and increased political pluralism desired by some progressive forces who advocate it. They tend to make extravagant claims that PR would act as a vehicle for a new kind of politics, allowing people to organise into groups which more closely reflect their own beliefs or interests, and undermining the power of the big party bureaucracies. Such claims

73

involve a great deal of wishful thinking and rhetorical argument; they are never substantiated, merely asserted.

A cooler examination of the evidence suggests it is more likely that the pattern of British politics would remain fixed around the three major political forces, with the centre-right probably re-aligning into a new position of dominance. If the *democratic* case for PR were so overwhelming, the left would simply have to live with that outcome. But since it is not, why persist, particularly when these additional claims made for it are also illusory?

7

DEMOCRATIC ALTERNATIVES

Although many claim that we have one of the 'most democratic systems in the world', democratic progress can no longer – if it ever could – be taken for granted in Britain. Because our political system suffers from major weaknesses it is necessary to consider which democratic reforms are appropriate and, if any contribution should be made by electoral reform, whether the Alternative Vote system might not be preferable to proportional representation.

An important indicator of the health of a democracy is the extent to which its citizens play a part in the decision-making process. In Britain, citizen participation is confined to relatively few people. Part of the reason is widespread political apathy and ignorance. Civic education hardly exists and, where it does, 'politics' is avoided, except for anodyne descriptions of the structure of parliamentary government. Socialisation for work, for family responsibilities, for adult life, takes place in the home, the school and the media – but our culture does not socialise people to participate in political activity. Politics is seen as something undertaken on behalf of others by *professionals* (i.e. politicians). The citizen's role is a passive one, focussed on casting a vote at periodic elections.

Centralisation

The scope for public participation is also limited by Britain's highly centralised system of government, which has become much more so since Mrs Thatcher won office in 1979. Local government in particular has found its powers, previously limited enough, massively reduced by direct Whitehall controls over expenditure. Local councils elected to improve public services (for instance, by subsidising public transport) have found local democratic wishes overridden by central government. In this environment, the desire for greater public participation that surfaced in the 1960s has been thwarted: while 'town hall democracy', already remote enough from local communities, was itself being undermined, there was no hope of extending it downwards through neighbourhood councils and community groups.

Within the national system of government, power has been centralised to a considerable degree on the Prime Minister. In recent years, the tendency towards 'prime-ministerial' rather than 'cabinet' (let alone 'parliamentary') government has increased. A significant aspect of this power is exercised through prime-ministerial appointments, from Cabinet Ministers and top civil servants to the head of the BBC, and by patronage both inside Parliament and through the honours system.

Between 1945 and 1976, for example, seven prime ministers made 1,494 ministerial appointments (309 in the Cabinet, 1,185 outside); created 568 hereditary and life peers, 118 baronetcies and 264 knighthoods; appointed 85 chairs of nationalised industries and 35 chairs of royal commissions. During this 31-year period, these same seven men also appointed hundreds of civil service permanent secretaries, ambassadors, chiefs of staff, and heads of the security services. Given that there may be two or three hopefuls for every successful candidate for an honour or appointment, prime-ministerial influence extended to between 5,000 and 7,000 senior people in public life: 'no medieval monarch could compare with it, either in numbers or in importance.'[80]

One of the major tools of the Prime Minister in particular and ministers and civil servants in general is extensive secrecy. British government is one of the most secretive in the world, the catch-all Section 2 of the Official Secrets Act being manipulated and frequently abused to control the flow of information vital to a healthy democracy. The contrast between the prosecution of civil servants Sarah Tisdall and Clive Ponting in 1984 and 1985 for leaking information embarassing to the Thatcher government, and the deliberate official leak of a confidential law officer's letter to a fellow member of the Cabinet in the Westland affair in 1986 showed how secrecy could be deployed in a politically discriminatory fashion.

Elitism, class and democracy

Britain is an elitist society. Senior posts in the civil service, the judiciary, and the military are generally occupied by people from a narrow upper-class, public-school background. Wealth and family status are still important tickets to education, opportunity, work and high living standards. Such elitism flows from the still deeply entrenched class structure which is the main source of inequality. There is a 'dominant' and a 'subordinate' class, people being divided mainly according to whether or not they own capital.[81] There are also other important sources of inequality – notably between men and women – which are only loosely connected to the basic class divide and indeed act within classes.

Inequalities of class, sex and race have placed severe limitations on democratic and individual freedom for the majority of the people. Only the minority of white, male members of the dominant class enjoy full democratic rights and real freedom.

Britain's class system has also had a deadening impact upon industrial relations. It reinforces old practices and anachronistic cultural behaviour. It blocks opportunities for workers to contribute their own ideas and skills to the running of their enterprises. It breeds conflict between employee and employer. By acting as a barrier against individual advance and self-development regardless of background, class inequalities have encouraged the 'industrial backwardness' which has been such a marked feature of Britain's steady economic decline.[82]

The first reason for extending democracy is that individual freedom cannot be protected if power is concentrated in a few hands. Second, each citizen has a fundamental right to a say in decisions affecting him or her. Third, the absence of democracy thwarts the development of human potential. Fourth, it affects the capacity of a society to prosper: democracy is arguably a necessary condition for sustained economic progress and for efficient use of resources.[83] Therefore, contrary to the views of many on the right and some on the left, democracy is not simply a means to an end, but an end in itself: it is essential on moral, political and economic grounds.

Indeed, the deeper democracy penetrates throughout society, the better – not just in government, but in industry, the City, large corporations and the financial institutions too. The only major constraints should be practicality and the balancing of the general interest against those of specific groups, local concerns or minority views.

The case against Britain's political system is not simply that it fails to achieve high democratic standards. By discouraging participation throughout society, particularly industrial democracy, it stifles individual initiative and energy and thereby acts as a brake on the country's ability to adapt to change, on its economic performance and ultimately on its prosperity.

Britain's parliamentary democracy

Support for this system is based on a number of conservative and mistaken assumptions. The first of these is the assumption that Parliament sits at the apex of real power in Britain. In fact, it is only one actor on the stage. It is severely constrained by a series of 'extra-parliamentary' forces, the most important being national and international private capital, which exercises massive power and shapes the whole nature of society. Parliament cannot easily resist the pressures of the industrial and financial elites which control private capital, as even the most radical Labour government ministers have discovered to their cost over the years.

A second assumption behind Britain's parliamentary democracy is that the state itself is a neutral body which can be steered in any direction according to the policies adopted by the party in office. In fact, in a capitalist society such as Britain's, the state operates within a wider division of power imposed by the class structure and cannot remain neutral as between these conflicting class interests: it usually tends to reflect the interests of the dominant class. The various agencies which make up the state – the civil service, judiciary, police and military – also reflect this class bias and, in addition, have their own interests to defend.

This is why even the most progressively reformers will end up failing if they assume – as, for example, all Labour governments have done – that the overriding purpose is to win elections and secure office, without actively engaging the support of sympathetic extra-parliamentary forces to resist the hostile forces of big business, bureaucracy and technology.

However, notwithstanding its shortcomings, Parliament is the principal, legitimate vehicle for democratic change in Britain and is seen as such by the vast majority of the population, who will oppose any group seeking to by-pass or overthrow it. Although the democratic process in Britain is limited, any attempt to override it will be rightly rejected as authoritarian and elitist.

Because of this, achieving the radical changes necessary in Britain will require the adoption of a 'third road' strategy, fusing parliamentary initiatives with the pressure which can be brought by the activity of progressive extra-parliamentary movements, including trade unions, women's groups, community associations and peace organisations.[84]

Participatory democracy

In place of the limited form of democracy inherent in the British system, the objective should be to create a 'participatory democracy' in which there is the greatest possible involvement of citizens. This will involve two principal changes: making representatives much more *accountable*; and *decentralising* decision-making as far as is compatible with wider interests.

However, power can only be spread downwards in an equitable manner if there is a national framework where opportunities, resources, wealth and income are distributed equally, where democratic rights are entrenched, and where there is sexual and racial equality.

If decentralisation were to be confined to government structures alone, it would simply reproduce the existing patterns of elitism and inequality at lower levels. The result would be a *dispersal of administration*, in which popular participation would still be blocked by the obstacles resulting from class, sex and race inequalities: the face of government would be more local, but it would not be more representative and would still be constrained by extra-parliamentary forces favouring the interests of dominant groups in society.

Effective decentralisation will require concentrations of private ownership and wealth to be broken up and spread more evenly throughout the population. It will mean national redistribution of resources from prosperous to poor regions of the country, from the suburbs to the inner cities, from the dominant to the subordinate classes, from rich to poor, from men to women, and from whites to blacks. There will need to be nationally established *minimum levels* of public provision. Minimum levels should be set for housing provision, public-transport subsidies, social services, nursery schools, day-care facilities, home helps and so on. There should also be a statutory minimum wage.

In addition, democracy can only be extended if there is social ownership and democratic control of the economy, because this is necessary to ensure that capital serves the interests of the majority of people and not the other way around. Government intervention and controls are essential in order to direct investment, to overcome the vagaries and injustices of market forces, to plan, and to secure economic progress in the interests of the majority.

But this need not mean the 'statist' approach (often identified with socialists in the past), according to which inequalities of power are overcome by the state, rather than the people involved, taking control. However worthy its intentions, this has led in practice to centralised bureaucracies suffocating local initiative and reproducing hierarchical structures. Policies and programmes implemented through the state are necessary to

80

clear away obstacles to democratic participation and freedom, but unless pressure is actively maintained through new democratic avenues from below, a participatory democracy will not *take root*.

There are severe limits on what can be achieved by a 'top down' focus on spreading power. National and local government can facilitate wider democracy. They can assist people to take greater control over their own lives. But government cannot force a participatory democracy onto people. Unless citizens have themselves participated in the process of gaining influence and pressing for greater control, they will not be prepared to take the new opportunities or exercise the extra responsibilities that go with increased decentralisation.

What sort of changes would be necessary to create a more participatory democracy? It is beyond the scope of this book to describe in detail how power could be devolved, and the purpose of this chapter is simply to show that there is a democratic alternative to the route mapped out by the main lobby for PR. But it is possible to outline the main reforms needed.

Parliamentary reform

To begin with, Parliament needs radically reforming. A combination of prime-ministerial control, the bureaucratic power of the civil service, institutional anachronisms in the House of Commons and the undemocratic blocking powers of the unelected House of Lords means that Parliament does not properly fulfil its democratic function. Constitutional theory about the legislature having control over the executive does not describe reality in Britain. Parliament usually rubber-stamps the wishes of government. The average backbench MP has very little power – far less than the average Chair of a local council committee.

Reforms should be directed at increasing the accountability of the executive to Parliament. The Lords should be abolished and its powers transferred to the Commons. Far from diminishing democracy, this would enhance it, as the powers of the Commons need strengthening.

Bills could be better scrutinised by altering the procedures for handling them, thus overcoming the argument that only the Lords provides a means of checking bad drafting. Standing Committees would have the opportunity to examine Bills and call witnesses before they were put before the floor of the House. After the Report Stage and before the final vote, a special Revision Committee could take another look to check for drafting errors and accommodate other improvements.

The system of Select Committees needs to be enhanced, giving them more powers, greater access to information and much better facilities and back-up resources, so that they can really maintain a close eye on the operations of each department of government.

The sheer weight of parliamentary business and the complexity of modern legislation mean that most MPs cannot possibly understand the full implications of the laws they dutifully troop through the lobbies to vote for (or against). MPs also have a constituency case-load which has increased massively since the War. They are expected to be active on local issues and to play a part in national policy determination. Yet the resources MPs receive now are so inadequate that they cannot do their jobs effectively. MPs should be given decent secretarial, research and office facilities: increased *staff allowances* for MPs should be the priority, not boosting their personal salaries.

In addition, the Commons should have more regular working hours, so that MPs are discouraged from having other paid jobs and so that they are able to live more normal lives. Both these moves would bring MPs closer to the people who elect them. Women would benefit particularly, though there are many other changes necessary to achieve equality for women MPs, such as introducing child-care facilities and scrapping the various antiquated routines which are modelled more on a gentleman's club than a genuinely representative parliament of the nation.

Even more substantial reforms are necessary to act as a counterweight against the power of Prime Ministers over their parliamentary parties. At present, Prime Ministers and their senior civil servants can prevent open discussion of decisions and policies by controlling the flow of information and invoking the protection of official secrecy. In the case of the Labour Party at least, there is already pressure for Labour MPs to elect Cabinet Ministers just as they elect the Shadow Cabinet – this would further undermine arbitrary prime-ministerial patronage and power.

The objective should be to make ministers much more accountable to Parliament, to their parties and, beyond that, to groups and opinions outside the parliamentary arena. One way of achieving this would be to have a system of 'ministerial committees' (consisting of MPs elected by their parliamentary party's specialist groups) to act as advisers to ministers and to provide a channel for support and consultation to and from the party as a whole.

More full-time political aides are needed in ministers' private offices to provide alternative advice and to act as watchdogs when civil servants are tempted to impede the implementation of radical policies. They should also have a 'campaigning role' in keeping open channels of communication between Whitehall and groups and individuals who have no access to senior policy-makers.

The complementary objective of building links with extra-parliamentary forces would be to challenge and overcome the financial, bureaucratic and political establishments, which will otherwise imprison even the best-intentioned minister. There has been a tendency to mistake being in *office* with being in *power*. In reality, there are enormous constraints on any government seeking radical reforms. Preoccupied with the time-consuming process of administration and legislative change, not enough attention has been given to using the machinery of government to mobilise popular support for radical policies.

Public servants

Ministerial appointments, heads of nationalised industries, senior civil servants and other major public appointments would need to be endorsed by Select Committees shadowing Government Departments, with such endorsements submitted for acceptance to the Commons as a whole. The many other public appointments now made from what almost seems like a list of 'the great and the good' ought to be made in a more open way. Positions should be advertised wherever possible, and nominations openly invited from the appropriate representative bodies. The procedure for appointing senior officers in the armed forces and the police also needs to be made democratically accountable.

Positive action is needed to correct the gross imbalance in appointments which has produced a judiciary disproportionately right-wing, upper-class, male and white. At present, judges are selected by the Lord Chancellor after recommendations from a legal profession which regulates itself and is not democratically accountable. Similarly, magistrates are chosen by the Lord Chancellor acting upon recommendations from local Advisory Committees whom he appoints and whose membership is a secret.

The security services should be made much more accountable. In the absence of any clear statutory basis for defining their duties and responsibilities, they have virtually become a law unto themselves. A Security Act should be introduced establishing the powers under which the security services operate and defining the meaning of terms such as 'subversion' (whose present ambiguity allows far too much discretion to be exercised and has led to serious infringements of individual rights). Parliament should receive an annual report on their operations, and a Select Committee on Security Services should be established to monitor their activities. Other steps include extending the rights of MPs to receive answers to parliamentary questions (which are often blocked at present) and permitting much more scrutiny of expenditure (also currently denied).

But the prerequisite to democratic accountability is information. The principle of open government should be enshrined in a Freedom of Information Act giving the public basic rights to information. This would replace the now discredited Official Secrets Acts.

Devolving power

However, very little will be achieved if reforms are concentrated at the centre. The overriding objective must be to devolve decision-making down through the structure of government, in order both to enhance democratic rights and to produce the better decisions which are likely to follow when the people most closely affected are involved.

Within such a framework, directly elected assemblies should be established in Scotland and Wales, not only with significant political powers but with significant industrial and economic ones as well.

In England, a system of regional government should be established. The gap between local authorities and national government has been made wider by Mrs Thatcher's abolition of the metropolitan authorities. Rather than simply reviving these, it would be more logical to abolish county councils as well and place a tier of regional authorities in between local and national levels. The new regional authorities should be given significant powers over economic planning and industrial intervention, as well as responsibility for strategic areas of policy such as town and country planning, the environment, health and transport.

As with other forms of decentralisation, control should be exercised through elected and accountable authorities, sweeping away the whole gamut of quangos and quasi-public institutions (now run by Whitehall appointees) and either taking over their functions or making them democratically accountable.

Local government

Local councils, too, should be given greater powers. Within district boundaries, they should have extensive powers of intervention in commerce and industry and should be able to sponsor local economic initiatives. They should also be given complete control over spending their own revenue provided they achieve minimum national standards. The centralised controls over rates and expenditure introduced by the Thatcher government will need to be abolished. In the longer term, the aim should be to introduce a new structure of local-government finance based on a local income tax and complemented by a nationally redistributive system of government grants given according to local need. This will be a fairer basis upon which to raise local revenue and will give local authorities more independence from central control.

Local-authority facilities should be opened up for more active use by local people, and community groups should be given greater information and access to the decision-making process. In this respect, the style of local government pioneered by radical Labour councils like the GLC in 1981-6 should be a model. There should also be a systematic decentralisation of services to administrative units outside the town hall. For example, neighbourhood housing offices should be established on council estates and tenants' associations given some control over their operations.

An 'alternative state'

In order to create structures through which participation can occur from below, the idea of an 'alternative state' should be pursued: a publicly resourced yet independent network established specifically to agitate against the dominant structures, whether these be traditional national structures or new local ones, and whatever political party happens to hold office.

Resources should be provided for community groups, tenants' associations, residents' groups, consumer groups, shop stewards' committees and so forth, enabling them to organise better and sustain their activity. Pressure on conventional structures – even if they happen to be controlled by progressives – should be welcomed and indeed encouraged, not thwarted. A priority should be given to establishing 'community resource centres'. These could offer certain local-authority services at neighbourhood level, such as housing advisers, welfare rights workers, health workers, community workers. They could also offer facilities for local groups. These community resource centres could be managed by local groups and should

86

become vehicles for local people to exert their own political leverage. Their management committees could be answerable to elected 'neighbourhood councils'. It is important not to impose standardised, pre-ordained structures upon local communities which are diverse in so many ways. It is also important not to suffocate community groups with official finance and the bureaucratic procedures which usually come with it. On the other hand, neighbourhood councils must not become mere talking shops. They need access to resources if there is to be any real decentralisation of democracy.[85] And this is why local authorities must be prepared to fund new structures such as community resource centres without insisting on the kind of bureaucratic control which so often alienates people who wish to become more involved in local issues.

Popular participation

To underpin such reforms of the structure of government and public administration, a sea-change in individual attitudes and aspirations will be needed. Otherwise, even the best-designed participatory system will founder on the rocks of apathy and public passivity.

The argument here is not that people should be *forced* to 'participate'. Nor is it suggested that their lives should be turned into an endless series of committee meetings. Instead, society should be consciously organised so as positively to promote and encourage popular participation by opening up the structures of power and by equipping people with the confidence and knowledge to take advantage of the new opportunities thereby created if *they* wish. At present they have little choice: only the most dedicated and confident can participate effectively.

Official encouragement should be given to families to educate young children about their civic rights and their opportunities to participate. To build upon this, there should be a major drive in the educational system and the media, and through subsidising 'public participation' training schemes. Instead of socialising for apathy, the socialisation process should encourage people to expect that they will be 'participators', that the positive exercise of their democratic rights is an important duty in their role as citizens. Experience suggests that a more participatory society is not merely more democratic, but is also healthier, since it has greater popular legitimacy.[86]

School pupils should have much greater rights over the management of their schools, students over their universities and colleges, consumers over the services they receive and the goods they purchase, pensioners over how and when they retire and the issues which affect them. This should apply to work as well, with industrial democracy encouraged by government legislation. Significantly, the evidence shows that workers are not only more content, but that their productivity is increased when they are given more control and a more direct say in the organisation and objectives of their work.[87]

So far this chapter has given a series of signposts showing where changes are necessary to defend and extend democracy. One of the problems with the case for proportional representation is that it does not address the key issues which have been identified. Although it may not exclude the possibility of pressing separately for greater popular participation and decentralisation of power, it concentrates upon the wrong questions: on voting procedures rather than on shifting the balance of political power. In this way, PR advocates also pose *false priorities* for democratic reform: simply re-arranging electoral procedures would leave Britain's elitist system of parliamentary democracy intact.

But is there still a case for including electoral reform in an overall programme of democratic reform? Even if *proportional representation* is rejected for the reasons explained in earlier chapters, there are two reasons why electoral reform cannot easily be dismissed: first, Britain's traditional two-party system shows clear signs of decline (with the steady growth of a third force since 1951) and, second, a majority of the public seem to favour a change.

Decline in the two-party system

First-past-the-post is best suited to a party system in which there are two main alternatives. Yet this is no longer the case.

TABLE 1 – COMBINED TORY/LABOUR SUPPORT

	% of total vote	% of total electorate
1951	96.8	79.9
1955	96.1	73.8
1959	93.2	73.4
1964	87.5	67.4
1966	89.9	68.1
1970	89.5	64.4
1974	75.1	59.2
1974	75.0	54.7
1979	80.8	61.4
1983	70.0	50.1

As Table 1 shows, the Conservatives and Labour between them polled 97 per cent of the total vote in 1951; by 1983 this had fallen to 70 per cent. Furthermore, the two parties have not only lost ground in actual votes. Due to a declining turnout of voters, by 1983 they commanded between them the support of barely half the total electorate.

Britain has had a system of *three* major parties at least since the early 1970s, and each party has a large share of support – a situation which is historically unprecedented: the only other period (during the 1920s) with more than two major parties can now be seen as a one of transition from one type of two-party structure to another, with Labour taking over from the Liberals. This latest period shows no signs of being only a temporary process of re-alignment: three-party politics is likely to be a permanent feature of Britain's political landscape for the foreseeable future.

Another important trend has been the consistent inability of the system to produce a government supported by the majority of the people. From Table 2 it can be seen that since the Second World War the proportion of the electorate who got the government they voted for declined from just under 50

TABLE 2: RELATIONSHIP BETWEEN VOTES CAST AND
REPRESENTATION SECURED

	% of electors who got the government they voted for	number of seats won on a minority vote
1951	48.0	39
1955	49.7	37
1959	49.4	80
1964	44.1	232
1966	48.0	185
1970	46.4	124
1974	37.2	408
1979	43.9	206
1983	42.4	336

per cent in the 1950s to as low as 37 per cent in February
1974. Another measure of the trend was that the House of
Commons in 1983 had over four times as many MPs elected
on a *minority* vote as the Commons in 1959 and nearly nine
times as many as in 1951. In 1983, under half of the electorate
got an MP for whom they had voted.

Popular opinion and PR

Perhaps not surprisingly, therefore, support for electoral reform has grown. Over the past decade the majority specifically
backing proportional representation in opinion polls has varied
from 2:1 to 3:1. The highest support recorded was in March
1974, just after the fall of the Heath Government, when it
stood at 70 per cent.

In November 1985 Gallup asked the question 'Do you favour
a change to proportional representation?' and found: YES: 59%;
NO: 20%; DON'T KNOW: 21%. However, this approval of the
idea of PR was not as straightforward as it may seem. The
same poll asked the same people about the present system and
found 58 per cent 'Very or fairly satisfied' and only 31 per
cent 'Not very or not at all satisfied'. (Even 47 per cent of
SDP/Liberal Alliance supporters expressed themselves 'very
or fairly satisfied' with the existing first-past-the-post system.)

A further question about what priority should be given to changing the electoral system elicited the response that only 22 per cent thought it 'very important' (in a June 1983 Gallup poll the figure was 29 per cent.)

What does this evidence, combined with the analysis in previous chapters, suggest? First, while a majority of the public favour the principle, they still have to be convinced that PR would be an improvement on the present system and believe that other issues – tackling unemployment, for example – are far more important. Second, while the undoubted shortcomings of first-past-the-post mean there is a case for *electoral reform*, the case for *proportional representation* is much weaker.

So, is there a better way of improving Britain's electoral arrangements than those already canvassed? Can the desire for electoral reform be accommodated in a way that overcomes the democratic disadvantages of PR?

The Alternative Vote

One option is the Alternative Vote, which is used in the Australian House of Representatives and retains single-member constituencies like the present ones. Rather than placing a mark against a single name, each voter numbers the candidates listed on the ballot paper in order of preference (e.g. 1st: Labour; 2nd: Liberal; 3rd: Conservative).

If any candidate achieves an overall majority right away (i.e more than half the first preferences of voters on the first count), then he or she is elected. If not, the candidate with the lowest number of first votes is eliminated and the second preferences of voters for him or her are allocated to the other candidates as indicated. This process is repeated through later counts, with bottom candidates falling out at each stage and their votes allocated to those remaining until one of these achieves an overall majority.

There is no obligation upon voters to indicate any specific number of preferences. In 'safe' seats dominated by one party, it is likely that the supporters of that party at least would vote for it and express no later preferences. In marginal seats it is more likely that voters would express their second or third preferences (though again they need not do so): in this way, even if they could not secure the victory of the party they strongly supported, they could try to block the one they most strongly opposed.

Consider, for example, a typical marginal seat. In the 1983 general election the result might have been something like this:

Conservative:	21,000 (46%)
Labour:	17,000 (37%)
Alliance:	8,000 (17%)

In other words, the Tory won with a 9 per cent majority of 4,000 votes. Supposing Alliance voters had indicated overwhelmingly that their second preference was for Labour, then the Labour candidate would have won. On the other hand, the second preferences of Alliance supporters might have split 60:40 to Labour and the Tories respectively, in which case the Tory would still have won, albeit with a majority only half that in the 'actual' 1983 result.

What effect, then, would the AV have had on the 1983 general election as a whole? A computer-based analysis done by Peter Kellner in the *New Statesman* showed that the Tories would still have won, despite having been the first choice of just 42 per cent of voters, but with a much smaller majority and with the Alliance more than doubling its share of seats.[88]

It was assumed that everyone cast their first-preference votes for the party they actually supported on the day (even though in reality this might not happen). The impact of minor-party candidates' later preferences was ignored in the analysis. Then different results were predicted on the basis of several different further assumptions.

The first and most simple (option 'A') was that wherever Labour or Tories came third, the second preferences of their supporters would all transfer to the Alliance, and wherever the Alliance came third, their supporters' second preferences would divide equally between the other two parties.

The second option ('B') was that the Alliance would only pick up 80 per cent and not all the second preferences of third-placed Labour or Tory candidates, with third-placed Alliance supporters dividing 60-40 in the Tories' favour.

The third option ('C') followed the 80 per cent transfer to the Alliance from Labour or Tory candidates coming third, but assumed a 50:50 division of losing Alliance supporters to the others.

The fourth ('D') also followed the 80 per cent transfer but this time assumed a 60:40 division of Alliance supporters in favour of Labour.

The outcome predicted for 1983 was as follows:

	Actual Result	Alternative Vote Options			
		'A'	'B'	'C'	'D'
Conservative:	397	349	389	368	344
Labour:	209	194	179	200	224
Liberal:	17	44	33	33	33
SDP:	6	44	30	30	30

Disadvantages of the AV

Despite securing a fairer relationship between seats and votes, the AV is strongly opposed by supporters of PR for a number of reasons. First of all, it is not a proportional system: it may be fairer than the existing system, but it does not achieve the degree of proportionality of List or STV systems. Because the AV retains single-member seats there is not 'room' for the spread of representation found in multi-member seats or on Lists.

It also suffers from a number of anomalies which have led PR supporters to argue that it 'is an inherently capricious mode of correcting the inequities' of the first-past-the-post system.[89] In certain circumstances, they point out, results can be unrepresentative, from 'the comparatively mild distortion' of the 1966 election in Australia (when the Liberal-Country Party alliance won a large parliamentary majority on a tiny majority of the popular vote), to the 'extreme exaggeration' of the 1948 Canadian election in the province of Alberta (where one party won *all* the seats with 58 per cent) and the 'absurdity' of the election in the Australian state of Victoria in 1967 (when the Liberals won three times as many seats as Labour despite having fewer first-preference votes).[90] However, the Australian examples were peculiar to the country's party structure; whether these anomalies could occur in Britain with its system of large national parties and its bigger electorate, is much less certain.

In three-cornered fights, the AV could produce winners with little more than a third of first-preference votes. The Alliance would be the main beneficiary in the political climate which has established itself since the early 1970s and could even gain a freak majority of MPs through coming second in first preferences more often than the other parties. This is because, whilst support for the Alliance is not as deep as for Labour or the Tories, it is potentially wider. The AV can favour candidates for the negative reason that they generate least opposition, rather than the positive one that they command solid support.

In this way the AV can produce what might be called 'lowest common denominator' MPs – ones to whom people take least exception or to whom they will give their second preferences in order to block Labour or the Tories. In June 1931, Churchill derided the AV as 'the worst of all possible plans' with an outcome 'determined by the most worthless votes given to the most worthless candidates.'[91] But that ringing denunciation could be directed at PR systems as well, since the transferable vote favours candidates to whom there is least objection whether the seats are single- or multi-member.

Advantages of the AV

The *main* advantage of the AV over the existing system is that it requires winning candidates to secure a majority of votes, and this is a major if not complete step towards meeting the criticisms made by PR supporters. It would avoid indefensible anomalies such as the October 1974 result in Dumbartonshire East (where, in a four-cornered fight, the Scottish Nationalist won with 31.2 per cent, over 31.1 per cent for the Tory and 30.3 per cent for Labour; the Liberal got 7.3 per cent). In 1983, less than half the MPs were elected with a majority of

94

the vote: 336 (out of 650) won on a minority vote, 70 of these with less than 40 per cent. In February 1974 the discrepancy was even greater: nearly two-thirds of MPs (408) won on less than half the vote.

Second, there would be no fear of 'splitting the vote', so electors' first preferences could be more truly stated and would be a more reliable guide to their real views than currently, when some will vote to keep a particular party out. The problem of the 'wasted vote' would thus be overcome.

Third, it would undermine the tendency of the current system to concentrate party representation on a geographical basis, either between North and South or between cities and rural areas. In 1983, for example, the Tories won 54.2 per cent of votes in the South-East of England (excluding Greater London) and secured 106 seats, whereas Labour and the Alliance (with 45.1 per cent between them) secured just one seat each; conversely, in the City of Liverpool the Tories won 30 per cent of the vote but no seats at all.

Fourth, it would stop the kind of 'exaggerated' parliamentary majorities the Tories achieved in 1970, 1979 and 1983 by being much less biased against the Alliance.

Fifth, it would be easier than under PR to form majority governments, though coalitions would be more likely than under the current system.

Sixth, it would be easier to understand than STV and much simpler to introduce. The existing constituencies could be retained, with only the ballot paper, method of voting and counting altered.

Seventh, it would be a good system for by-elections, giving a more accurate picture of public attitudes to the government's policies than the existing system (it would probably be used for by-elections under STV as well, where only one MP in a multi-member seat needed replacing).

Eighth, and most important, the single-member constituency would remain. This would overcome the central democratic objections to PR and maintain local accountability to the community and to party members.

Effects of the AV in Britain

It is difficult to be certain about its effect on the balance of party representation. In the longer term, the AV might well alter electoral behaviour in a radical fashion, and in ways it is not easy to foresee. In the short term, the Alliance would benefit most, since in 1983 it was placed second in by far the most seats (313). Since the majority of these were Tory (265), the Tories could lose more than Labour from the AV, at least in the immediate future.

The AV would penalise Labour less than the Tories in other ways. Labour could well benefit more in its 'target' marginal seats, since most of these are in urban areas where a larger proportion of Alliance voters could be expected to switch to Labour. Assuming a recovery in the Labour vote from the depths of 1983, even if the party's prospects of forming a majority government would be reduced under the AV, the Tories' prospects for doing so would be even dimmer. Unless it falls back to its 1983 level of support, Labour is likely to secure the largest number of seats more easily than the Tories in a three-party system accentuated by the AV. The main consolation for the Tories is that they would be more able to form a coalition with the Alliance to block socialist measures.

In its own internal party elections, Labour already practises something akin to the AV. An 'eliminating-ballot' procedure is used for national leader and local officer elections: bottom candidates fall out and further ballots are held until one candidate obtains an overall majority. The AV is a compressed version of this.

Given the history of electoral reform in Britain, it is hard to envisage the AV being introduced free from partisan motives. It is also open to the major reservation applied to PR: other democratic reforms are far more important. Nevertheless, there is a strong case for the AV in elections to Parliament, local councils, Scottish and Welsh Assemblies and regional authorities in England – a much stronger one, certainly, than that for the STV or List options.

European elections

But elections to the European Assembly are a different matter. Here most of the objections to STV do not apply.

The argument about local democracy and accountability is hardly relevant in a situation where there are 81 European MPs, each having a constituency of about 500,000 electors. The case for fair representation becomes overwhelming, especially since the 1984 EEC elections: the Alliance polled 19 per cent yet won no seats at all. The Tories benefited most from the present system by polling 41 per cent and winning 45 seats. Labour polled 37 per cent and won 32 seats. (The Scottish Nationalists won 1, and 3 were elected from Northern Ireland.) Under a proportional system like STV, the Alliance would have won 15, the Tories 32 and Labour 30 seats.

The argument that first-past-the-post is better able to produce governments elected upon clear programmes is not relevant either. At present, and for the foreseeable future, the role of the European Parliament is not to form a government but to act as a forum for the representation of different views in Europe. STV is clearly well suited to doing that.

The most sensible reform would be to have STV in multi-member seats based upon the ten existing British Economic Regions. This has been suggested by a variety of bodies, including the National Committee for Electoral Reform and the Labour Study Group on Electoral Reform. Ten new multi-member constituencies could then be formed within those regions by amalgamating existing parliamentary seats much as has been the case under EEC elections to date, except on a larger basis, as shown in the accompanying table.

In the 1984 EEC election, the 3 MPs from Northern Ireland were actually chosen by STV in one multi-member seat covering the whole area, showing that the proposal is quite feasible.

Conclusion

If there is no return to a two-party system, then the pressure for some sort of change in the voting system could become

Seats	Number of MEPs
SOUTH EAST	
Greater London, Essex, Beds, Bucks, Oxon, Berks, Hants, Wight, Surrey, Kent, East and West Sussex	24
SOUTH WEST	
Dorset, Wilts, Glos, Avon, Soms, Devon	6
EAST ANGLIA & EAST MIDLANDS	
Suffolk, Norfolk, Cambs, N'hants, Leics, Lincs, Notts, Derbys	8
WEST MIDLANDS	
W. Midlands, Warwicks, Staffs, Salop, Herefords, Worcs	7
NORTH WEST	
Greater Manchester, Cheshire, Mersey, Lancs	9
YORKSHIRE & HUMBERSIDE	
S.Yorks, W.Yorks, N. Yorks, Humber	7
NORTH	
Cleveland, Durham, Cumbria, Tyne & Wear, Northumberland	5
WALES	4
SCOTLAND	8
NORTHERN IRELAND	3

overwhelming. But a basic question still needs to be asked: what actual difference to the lives of the majority of people would electoral reform make? The answer is, surely: not very much. A far more fruitful approach by those serious about radical change would be to transform the whole antiquated and elitist structure of British government into one that is open, participatory and re-distributes the maximum possible power to every citizen. This – with the optional extra of the AV in domestic elections and STV for EEC elections – is the positive, democratic alternative to the case for proportional representation in Britain.

APPENDIX: THE COUNTING PROCEDURE UNDER STV

The counting procedure under STV is quite complex, although this extract from Joe Rogaly's *Parliament for the People* (Temple Smith, 1976) describes it in a readable way (he uses the term 'supervote' interchangeably with STV):

The first step is natural: the votes are added up. The Returning Officer will be in the counting-hall just like the ones that have become so familiar in TV General Election reports. The piles of votes will be visible on the long rows of tables, with the counting clerks standing, or sitting, by them and the party agents wandering around the hall. Say the number of votes cast in Beckenham-Croydon is announced as 213,993, the October 1974 total. Seventeen candidates have taken part (there were fifteen from the main parties in October 1974, plus two fringe candidates) and there are five seats to fill.

The second step is also natural. The votes are sorted according to first preferences. Your super-vote will be in the pile belonging to the candidate against whose name you wrote '1' on the ballot paper.

If the same candidates received the same number of votes as they did in October 1974, the sheet would look as shown on p. 100.

The third step does not come quite so naturally. The Returning Officer has to work out a *quota* of votes – that is, just how many votes each of the five winning candidates must have if he or she is to be declared a winner. Since it is a fair-shares system, this quota must be the same for each candidate, with the lowest possible number of votes left over, or 'wasted'.

Croydon-Beckenham; seats: 5; candidates: 17
Total votes cast: 213,993

Conservatives

Clark, W. G.	25,703	
Moore, J.E.M.	20,390	
Goodhart, P.C.	19,798	
Weatherill, B.B.	17,938	
Taylor, R.G.	16,035	Total 99,864

Labour

Winnick, D.	20,226	
Simpson, D.	15,787	
Boden, S.J.	14,556	
Sharp, N.J.	11,140	
Keene, D.W.	7,203	Total 68,912

Liberal

Nunneley, D.	11,514	
Mitchell, G.D.	10,578	
Maxwell, I.H.	7,834	
Streeter, P.T.	7,228	
Pitt, W.H.	6,563	Total 43,717

Other

Holland P. (National Front)	1,049
Stringer, W. (Independent British Nationalist)	451

The formula used in super-vote counts for establishing the quota is: first divide the number of votes cast by the number of seats to be filled, plus one. That comes to 213,993 divided by 6=35,665. But if every candidate received just that many votes you would of course have elected six MPs instead of five. So the quota is increased by one – and becomes 35,666. The full reasoning behind this formula is explained later: the essential principle is that it produces the lowest number of votes necessary to elect each of five candidates, with the smallest number of votes wasted.

The fourth step is easy: you look down the list to see if any of the candidates has enough first-preference votes to make up the quota. The list above shows that in this particular election not one of the candidates can make it at this stage.

The ice-tray has many cubes with too little water in them; none is full. The Returning Officer has to make some transfers.

The fifth step follows perfectly logically. The votes of the hopeless cases are transferred. On the list above you would take Stringer first, then Holland, then Pitt, Keene, and Streeter. The votes of each would be transferred in turn. They would whizz across to the piles of other candidates according to the 2 marks written on them. You might have voted 1 for Pitt and 2 for Nunneley; your super-vote goes to help Nunneley. Or it might be 1 for Keene, 2 for Simpson – up goes the super-vote. Each time a transfer is made the pile of those who receive the second-choice votes grows a little larger. The ice-tray cubes are filling up. As soon as someone has the quota of 35,666 he or she is declared elected.

This avoids the wastage of votes cast for hopeless or losing candidates. But what about the wastage that might occur when *too many* votes are cast for a popular candidate? Say Clark had received 45,000 votes – 10,000 more than the quota. As a popular Tory he might have done so, at the expense of less popular colleagues. Or say some of the transfers from losing candidates put a leader over the top. What then?

The answer is that the Returning Officer transfers the extra votes to whichever candidates the voter has indicated. You might have voted for Clark on first preference, and he might have too many votes. Your super-vote will then move to help someone else – just who, depends on what you wrote on the ballot paper.

But, people rightly ask, how is it decided which of the votes in Clark's pile of votes are surplus? Which should move across? Votes are not really drops of water moving across to ice cubes; they may be different from one another. Your second choice may not be the same as that of other Clark supporters.

In fact your super-vote is given as fair a chance to move across to another pile as every other super-vote. This is done either by taking the last ('surplus') votes put on the pile, or by taking an arithmetical proportion of the second choices of all of Clark's voters. The two methods are explained in greater detail below.

And so the transfers are made, one at a time. Each time the pile of votes of a certain loser is eliminated the second or third or later choices of the people who voted for that loser get the benefit. Similarly, the surplus votes of a winner are spread about. This process goes on until five candidates each have 35,666 votes by their names made up of some first preferences for each of them, with usually some second, third or later preferences added on. This means that 5 times 35,666 votes, or 178,330 of the 213,993 were 'useful'.

There will be 35,663 votes over – and this 16.7 per cent of the vote will, alas, be wasted. But it is a great improvement on the wastage of 140,759 votes, or 65.7 per cent of those cast in the October 1974 election in the five separate X-vote seats taken to make up our imaginary maxi-constituency. This is a real figure, taken from the 1974 results. There were about 114,000 votes cast for Labour, Liberal, or fringe losing candidates, and a surplus of 26,630 votes cast for Conservatives who could have won without them.

Counting the super-vote: some details

The militant democrat does not need to know more about the super-vote count than has been set out in the above description. But for those who want to know, the two sets of further details promised above are as follows:

The quota

The idea is that at the end of the counting the piles of votes will be of more or less equal size, just as the ice cubes will all be full. So to work out a quota you ask just how many votes will be in each victor's pile at the end of the count if each one is to be of equal size.

There is a trap here. You might think, 'That is easy; just divide the total number of votes cast by the number of seats to be filled'. Well you *could* do it that way, and when the system was first invented that is the way it was proposed. But consider: if there was just one candidate in a single-member constituency, and you divided by one to get the quota, you would be saying that he or she needed all the votes to win! In fact in a race between two candidates just half the votes plus one would be enough. Work it out: if there were a hundred votes shared between two candidates, fifty-one would be the lowest number necessary to win. And forty-nine would be the lowest possible number of 'wasted' votes.

If the constituency had to return two members, and there were three candidates (the least you would need for a contest in this case), then the lowest number that each of the two winners would need would be one-third of the total vote plus one. The arithmetic proves the point. Say there are 99 votes cast (to make the division easy). Then if you divide the number of votes cast by the number of seats to be filled you get 49.5. So two of the candidates would have to get 49.5 votes each, and the third none. This is clearly wrong. Very well, divide by three – that is, one more than the number of seats to be filled. Then each candidate gets thirty-three votes – clearly a tie and wrong again. So make the quota just one more – 34. Then the least the two winners would need would be thirty-four votes each, while the most the loser could have would be thirty-one. The wasted vote would be down to just under one-third of the total.

And so it goes on. In a three-seat constituency, just one more than a quarter of the votes cast would be enough to win. That is, if there were a hundred votes cast, the least that each of the three winners would need would be twenty-six votes each, while the waste would be down to twenty-two votes.

The technical name for this simple calculation is the 'Droop quota', after its inventor, a Dutchman called H. R. Droop. It is fair game for those who want to use the chance to mock a funny foreign name as a means of argument; but once the militant democrat has heard the joke a few times he can continue.

The Droop quota can be expressed as a formula:

(Total number of votes) ÷ (Number of seats + 1) + 1 = Droop quota

So a constituency represented by five MPs for whom 960 votes are cast would have a Droop quota of 161. How? Divide the total number of votes (960) by the number of seats plus one (6) to get the answer, 160. Add one. Answer 161. If each one of the five winners landed up with 161 votes in his or her pile that would be 805 votes used and 155 votes, or less than 17 per cent, wasted. Thus the merit of the Droop quota is that by making sure that each candidate wins the smallest possible number of votes, the wastage is kept to a minimum.

If you wish, try the little test given in the British government's Northern Ireland pamphlet. Assume there are twenty-four children voting for three prefects. The answer – the Droop quota in their case – is given at the end of this Appendix.

The transfers

The transfer of the votes of the candidate who has least votes is easy enough to carry out. In Northern Ireland the ballot papers themselves are physically re-sorted and shifted over to the candidates on which the second or third or later preferences are marked.

But the transfer of the surplus votes of a candidate who has too many is not quite so simple. How do you decide which votes are to be moved? How do you decide which are to be super-votes?

There are several ways. One is to take the surplus votes from the most popular pile at random, and distribute them to the other candidates. This might be fair, on the ground that a random sample of opinion is usually a fair sample. Another more acceptable way is in fact used in the Republic of Ireland.

All the votes of the candidate with the votes to spare are re-sorted into little piles according to the '2' preferences on them. Some Returning Officers have a big bank of pigeon-holes ready for this re-sorting. Now the second choices of the supporters of that overpopular candidate can be seen, physically. Some of these second preference votes are then taken from each pile and sent along to the candidates indicated by the 2 marks on them. Which? The last to have been put in the pigeon-holes. How many? A fair share taken from each pigeon-hole until the unnecessary extra votes are used up. If the favourite had twice as many votes as he needed to reach his quota then half the votes would be taken from each second-preference pile and moved according to the voter's written instruction. The other half is enough for the quota. If the favourite had a third too many votes, then a third of the votes in each pigeon-hole would be transferred – and so on.

For some people even this is not certain enough to produce a fair result. The Northern Ireland Office pamphlet explains:

'Suppose the quota is 1,000 votes and candidate A gets 1,500 votes in the first count. That means 500 of his votes, a third of his total, are to be re-distributed as surplus. In the counting system used in the 1920s, the 1,500 ballot papers were examined to find out the proportion of second preferences for the other candidates, and then 500 ballot papers were taken at random to reflect that pattern, and distributed among other candidates.' This is something like the Southern Irish pigeon-hole method.

'Some people said "That's all very well, but how is anyone to be sure that the 500 papers transferred reflect faithfully the pattern of later preferences expressed by the 1,500 people who voted for candidate A? They don't matter now but they might become important later in the count." ' In other words every one of those 1,500 imaginary voters might have a slightly different order of preference. They have all chosen the same person as the candidate of their first choice, of course, but they will split up (and do in actual elections) in different directions for their second choices, and in different directions yet again for their third choices, and so on. The super-vote is above all personal.

It was to meet this obligation, says the pamphlet, that the

'senatorial rules' (so called because they were used to elect the senates of South Africa and both Northern and Southern Ireland) were introduced to the Northern Ireland general election.

'What happens is that instead of transferring one-third of the votes, all the 1,500 votes are transferred at one-third of their value. This does not mean that your vote is actually divided up. It is simply a mathematical way of ensuring that the value of 500 votes is transferred to the candidates to whom they are due in the proper proportion.'

Say one of the candidates, needing only 200 votes to win, has 300 votes in his or her pile. According to the senatorial rules, each of those 300 – the lot – will then be inspected for second preferences. Say they divide up 180 for one of the candidates, 120 for another. Then you would say to yourself – 'the number of extra votes was 100 out of 300 or one-third. Since 180 of them want to go to that other chap over there, he would have one-third of 180, or 60 votes accredited to him. And as 120 want that lady over there, she shall have one-third of 120, or 40 accredited to her.' In this way the 100 surplus votes will have been transferred. The same sums will be done all over again for third or later preferences. The Returning Officer will by this stage be thanking heaven for the modern calculating machines available to him.

The counting method of the super-vote, or single transferable vote, with its painstaking devices to ensure as much fairness as possible at every stage, is as simple, or if you like complicated, as that. When it is all completed the result will be declared in such a way that you can read off just what happened at each stage. The first column will show the names and parties of each candidate, the number of first-preference votes polled by each one, the total vote, and, at the top of the page, the quota.

The second column will show how the votes of, say, the lowest-scoring candidate have been transferred to all the others, with the new totals for each of them alongside. Then if someone is put over the top, the surplus votes (perhaps transferred by the senatorial rules) will be shared out among the others. The next column will show this, and the next one the new totals. It is just like a map of the collective mind of the electorate, on which you can read off just who each group fancies most, just who each candidate's supporters prefer as second best and so on.

(Answer to puzzle: the Droop quota is $24 \div 4 + 1 = 7$.)

REFERENCES

1. Vernon Bogdanor, *What is Proportional Representation?* (Martin Robertson, 1984), p. 142.
2. Rosaleen Hughes and Philip Whitehead, in *Electoral Reform* (Fabian Tract 483, September 1982), p.20. See also A.H.Birch, *Representative and responsible Government* (Allen & Unwin, 1972), pp. 62-3.
3. Elizabeth Lyon, *PR and Parliament: Round One 1866-1931* (Parliamentary Democracy Trust, 1979), p.2.
4. See ibid. for details of the debates in Parliament.
5. Michael Steed, 'The Evolution of the British Electoral System', in S. E. Finer (ed.), *Adversary Politics and Electoral Reform* (Anthony Wigram, 1975), pp. 47-8.
6. Ibid., p. 48.
7. Ibid., p. 49.
8. See, for example, Enid Lakeman, *How Democracies Vote* (Faber, 1974) and publications of the Electoral Reform Society, 6 Chancel Street, London SE1 0UX.
9. Report of the Hansard Society, *Commission on Electoral Reform* (June 1976), p.36.
10. Electoral Reform Society, *Electing the UK Parliament* (1976).
11. Joint Liberal/SDP Alliance Commission, *Electoral Reform* (July 1982).
12. See Vernon Bogdanor, *What is Proportional Representation?* (Martin Robertson, 1984), pp. 97-8.
13. Ibid., pp. 96, 98-9.
14. For a reliable guide, see Joe Rogaly, *Parliament for the*

People (Temple Smith, 1976), pp. 85-94.
15. *Guardian*, 2 February 1978.
16. Lakeman, op. cit., pp. 107-8
17. Giovanni Sartori, *Democratic Theory* (New York, Frederick Praeger, 1965), p. 252.
18. For a brief description, see Tony Benn, *Arguments for Democracy* (Cape, 1981), pp. 186-7.
19. Evidence summarised by Ivor Crewe, 'Electoral Reform and the local MP', in Finer, op. cit., pp. 331-5.
20. Ibid., pp. 321-2.
21. Nevil Johnson, 'Adversary Politics and Electoral Reform: Need We be Afraid?', in Finer, op. cit., pp. 80-81.
22. Crewe, op. cit., p. 326.
23. Lakeman, op. cit., pp. 55-7.
24. Hughes and Whitehead, op. cit., pp. 22-3.
25. Lakeman, op. cit., pp. 111, 149, 152-3.
26. Crewe, op. cit., p. 340.
27. Sartori, op. cit., p. 107.
28. Hugh Berrington, 'Electoral Reform and National Government', in Finer, op. cit., p. 288.
29. Quoted in *New Statesman*, 3 April 1981.
30. Lakeman, op. cit., pp. 225-7.
31. See Peter Kellner, *New Statesman*, 3 April 1981.
32. Rogaly, op. cit., p. 91.
33. See William Hampton, *Democracy and Community* (Oxford University Press, 1970), pp. 106-12, and Royal Commission on Local Government in England, *Community Attitudes Survey* (HMSO, 1969), p. 15.
34. Bogdanor, op. cit., pp. 155-6.
35. A. B. Atkinson, *Unequal Shares* (Penguin, 1974), p. 31.
36. Michael Steed, 'The Evolution of the British Electoral System', in Finer, op. cit., p. 41.
37. Nicholas Clarke, *The Story of the Great Vote Robbery* (Liberal Group for Electoral Reform, 1975), p. 17.
38. *Guardian*, 10 September 1985.
39. Berrington, op. cit., p. 291.
40. David Owen, *Face the Future* (Cape, 1981), p. 114.
41. Ibid., pp. 345-51.
42. *New Statesman*, 3 April 1981.

43. Shirley Williams, *Politics is for People* (Penguin, 1981).
44. *New Statesman*, 9 October 1981.
45. Nevil Johnson, op. cit., pp. 75-6.
46. Ibid., pp. 72-3.
47. Finer (ed.), op. cit., p. 29.
48. Ibid., pp. 30-1.
49. Ibid. p. 50.
50. See John Ross, *Thatcher and Friends* (Pluto, 1983).
51. *Guardian*, 21 January 1982.
52. *The Times*, 22 July 1981.
53. John Lawson, letter to the *Guardian*, 18 July 1984.
54. *The Times*, 23 November 1979.
55. 'Constitutional Reform Now' (Conservative Action for Electoral Reform).
56. Ibid.
57. 'Why Industry Needs Electoral Reform *Now*' (National Committee for Electoral Reform).
58. *Observer*, 19 June 1983.
59. Nicholas Clarke, op. cit., p. 21.
60. *Guardian*, 24 June 1981.
61. *Now!*, 21 December 1979.
62. *Guardian*, 9 September 1981.
63. Rogaly, op. cit., pp. 3-4.
64. See Elizabeth Lyon, op. cit., p. 9.
65. Ibid.
66. Labour Study Group on Electoral Reform, *Testing our Electoral System* (1976).
67. Labour Campaign for Electoral Reform (1979).
68. Keith Sharp, in *Representation*, No. 79, Vol.20 (Electoral Reform Society, April 1980).
69. Hansard Society, op. cit., para. 106.
70. Ken Livingstone in conversation with Tariq Ali, *Who's Afraid of Margaret Thatcher?* (Verso, 1984)
71. Michael Rustin, *For a Pluralist Socialism* (Verso, 1985), pp. 133-4.
72. Ibid., p. 140.
73. Ibid., p.143.
74. Dave Cook, 'PR: threat or opportunity?', *Marxism Today* (February 1983), p. 21. See also John Peck, *Proportional Rep-*

resentation (Communist Party, 1984).

75. Cook, op. cit., p. 22.

76. Barbara Rogers, *52%: Getting Women's Power into Politics* (The Women's Press, 1983), p. 172.

77. Bogdanor, op. cit., pp. 115-16.

78. Ibid., p. 115.

79. Cook, op. cit.

80. Tony Benn, op. cit., (Cape, 1981), pp. 27-8.

81. See Ralph Miliband, *Capitalist Democracy in Britain* (Oxford University Press, 1982), p. 5.

82. See Geoff Hodgson, *Labour at the Crossroads* (Martin Robertson, 1981).

83. See Geoff Hodgson, *The Democratic Economy* (Penguin, 1984).

84. The term 'third road strategy' has been coined by New Left activists in the Labour Party. See Peter Hain, *The Democratic Alternative* (Penguin, 1983), pp. 151-7.

85. For analysis of public participation and neighbourhood councils, see Peter Hain, *Neighbourhood Participation* (Temple Smith, 1980).

86. Carole Pateman, *Participation and Democratic Theory* (Cambridge University Press, 1970).

87. See Geoff Hodgson (1984), op. cit., especially pp. 135-9. See also P. Blumberg, *Industrial Democracy: the sociology of participation* (Constable, 1968), F. H. Stephen (ed.), *The Performance of Labour-Managed Firms* (Macmillan, 1982), D. C.Jones and J. Svejnar (eds.), *Participatory and Self-Managed Firms* (D. C. Heath & Co., Lexington, Mass., 1982).

88. *New Statesman*, 17 February 1984. For a similar analysis of the effect of the AV on the October 1974 result, see Berrington, op. cit., pp. 273-7.

89. For example, Berrington, op. cit., p. 277.

90. Enid Lakeman, op. cit., p. 67.

91. Quoted in Rogaly, op. cit., p.84.

INDEX

113